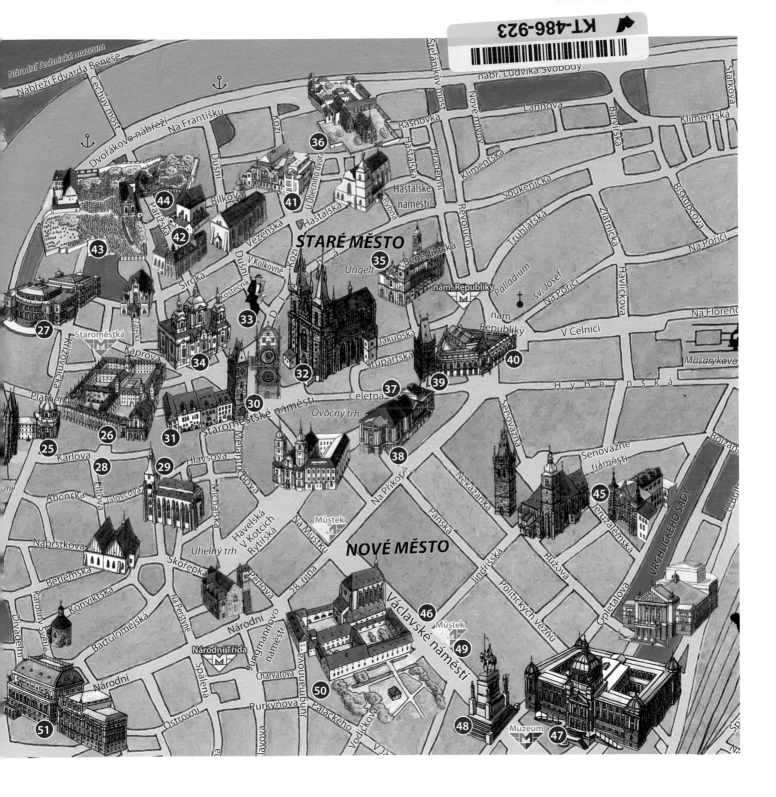

Following older settlements of tribes like the Celts and the Marcomanni, Slav tribes arrived at Vltava River valley around the 7th century. The first historically known Czech prince, Borivoj, converted to Christianity and moved his seat from Levy Hradec (Left Castle) to the area of Prague Castle. At the beginning of the 9th century, he established the Palace and Church of Virgin Mary in the area of Prague Castle.

In the first half of the 10th century, under the rule of Prince Wenceslas, the Rotunda of St Vitus was built where the cathedral stands today. During the reign of Prince Sobeslav a new princely palace was erected. We learn about the wealth and prosperity of the city from the 965 AD report by the Jewish-Arabic merchant Abraham ben Jacob. He refers to Prague as the stone city and he is impressed by the stone buildings at Prague Castle.

The original coat of arms of Prague

A view of the bridges over Vltava River from Hanavsky Pavilion in Letna

PRAGUE

the jewel in the heart of Europe

The golden city of a hundred spires,
the mother of cities, is today the capital of the Czech Republic
and with its beauty it attracts many visitors from all over the world.
This book can either serve as an invitation
to visit the magical city of Prague or as a memento of your visit.

PINTA

publisher
Daniel Pinta
Prague 2018

author: Ivan Henn
publisher: Daniel Pinta

ISBN 978-80-7528-011-4

CONTENTS

INTRODUCTION 6

PETRIN HILL 12

STRAHOV MONASTERY 14

LORETO 18

NEW WORLD 22

CASTLE DISTRICT 24

PRAGUE CASTLE 30

PRAGUE CASTLE – THE CROWN JEWELS 46

LESSER TOWN 56

KAMPA ISLAND 65

INFANT JESUS OF PRAGUE 66

CHARLES BRIDGE 68

OLD TOWN 74

OLD TOWN – THE ASTRONOMICAL CLOCK 82

JEWISH QUARTER 98

NEW TOWN 105

VYSEHRAD 120

AROUND THE HISTORICAL CITY CENTRE 126

MODERN BUILDINGS AFTER THE VELVET REVOLUTION 132

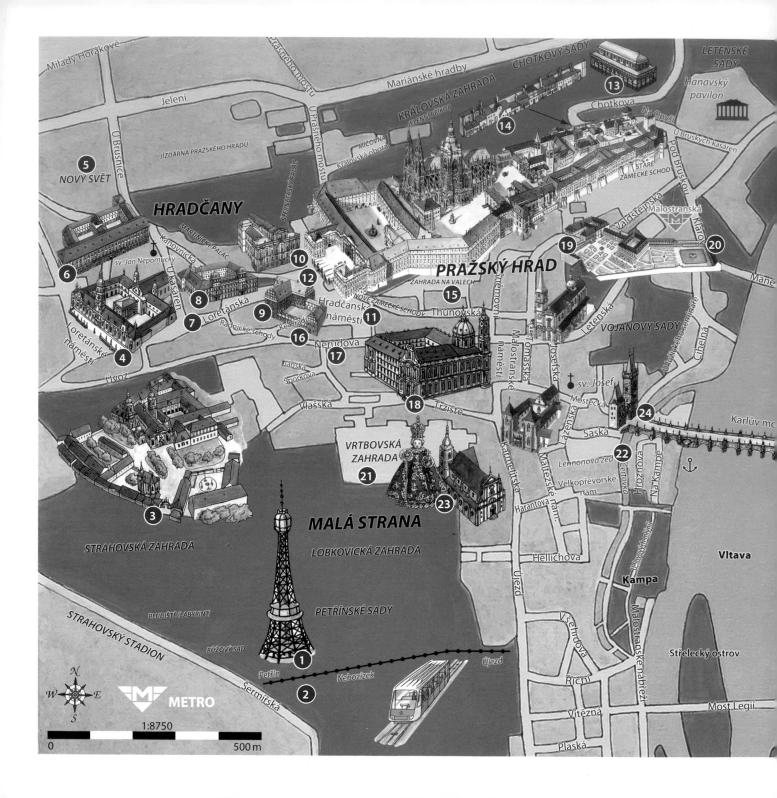

The growing centralisation of power under the reign of the Premyslids and the city's favourable position, led to its further development. The first monasteries in Prague were founded at the end of the 10th century and the Bisopric in 973.

In the 12th century, under the rule of Prince Vladislav II, the construction of a new palace at the Castle began, and its walls were fortified. A new stone bridge called Judith Bridge, named after Prince Vladislav's wife, connected the riverbanks. The bridge connected Prague Castle and its surroundings with the right bank of the river, which had been turning into an important centre of commerce since the 11th century.

The various settlements were gradually integrated under common administration. In 1257, during the rule of Premysl Ottokar II, New Town emerged at the foot of the Castle. It was later named Smaller Town of Prague and is now known as Lesser Town (Mala Strana). On the other bank, in Old Town, this process was completed in 1287.

The growing economical importance of Old Town, granted it the privilege of establishing the first town hall of the kingdom by King John of Luxembourg in 1338. In 1344, the same king laid the foundation stone of St Vitus Cathedral in Prague Castle. The Bishopric of Prague was elevated to Archbishopric, hence the need for a cathedral.

Holy Roman Emperor and King of Bohemia Charles IV ruled in the 14th century. After the death of his father, John of Luxembourg, the young ruler started transforming Prague based on his knowledge of big European cities. In 1348 he founded the first university in Central Europe, which to this day bears his name. He established New Town in the same year, which enclosed Old Town and also functioned as a protective zone. He built new city fortifications and after the destruction of Judith Bridge by floods, he commenced the construction of a new stone bridge over the river in 1357, which was later named Charles Bridge.

This period of prosperity was followed by a period of decline. The burning of priest Jan Hus at the stake for heresy in 1415 and the subsequent defenestration of the town councillors in New Town, mark the beginning of a revolution. This period of religious and social unrest, the Hussite Wars, interrupted the intense building development in the city. Old town and New Town of Prague were administratively unified for the time being and they contributed to the revolutionary movement. However, growing internal conflicts led to the defeat of the revolution at the final Battle of Lipany in 1434. In 1436, the son of Emperor Charles IV, Emperor Sigismund, arrived in Prague and as crowned Czech King attempted to re-establish order and to strengthen royal power. However, he was not welcome and he therefore quickly left the country. He died in Moravia during his return journey to Hungary. His successor, the elected King Albrecht of Habsburg, was also met with resistance. Stability was not introduced in the country even after the period of George of Podebrady's administration and the short reign of the young King Ladislaus Posthumus. In 1458, George of Podebrady was crowned King and he sought to reconcile political and religious groups, such as the Utraquists and the Catholics.

In Old Town Square, the Town Hall was rebuilt and expanded and the construction of the Church of Our Lady before Tyn was completed. In 1471 Vladislav II Jagiello was elected King and he enhanced royal power in the country. In the late 15th and early 16th floods, important buildings in Prague, such as the Vladislav Hall at Prague Castle and the Powder Tower in Old Town, started rising again.

In the early 16th century, the reign of the Jagiello kings ended and in 1526, Ferdinand I of Habsburg was elected King of Bohemia, starting the nearly four-hundred years of rule of Habsburgs in the country. Within the following period, remarkable Renaissance buildings were built in Prague, e.g. Palace of Queen Anne and Hvezda Summer Palaces. However, after the great fire of 1541 many of the older buildings were damaged. In Prague Castle, St Vitus Cathedral was damaged, the regional archives got burnt and the residences of Lesser Town were destroyed. The Renaissance style was dominant in the subsequent reconstruction and rebuilding of the city.

In the years 1583–1612, Prague was the seat of the court of Emperor Rudolf II of Habsburgs. As a cultural centre of the era, Prague greeted the arrival of eminent men, such as Tycho Brahe and Johannes Kepler. Rudolf II's Letter of Majesty in 1609, confirmed religious freedom. After the death of Rudolf II, Emperor Matthias moved back to Vienna in 1612 and once again disputes over religion and power emerged in the country, culminating in the Second Defenestration of Prague in 1618, when the Emperor's representatives were thrown out of a window of the Royal Palace. The

◄ *A view of Charles Bridge and Castle District from the Old Town Bridge Tower*

A view of Prague Castle and Lesser Town from Petrin Tower

uprising of non-Catholics uprising against the Habsburgs did not last for long. In 1620, at the Battle of White Mountain, the imperial troops defeated the Czech Estates army. Twenty seven leaders of the uprising were executed on the Old Town Square the following year. The defenestration marked the beginning of the Thirty Years' War, which had devastating consequences for the city, which was occupied by the Saxons while Prague Castle and Lesser Town were plundered by the Swedish. Paradoxically, this situation led to a spectacular Baroque reconstruction of the city that would last for more than a hundred years.

In all parts of the city, churches, monasteries, palaces of noblemen and other residences were being built or reconstructed in Baroque style. The construction work attracted local and foreign builders and artists to Prague. To this day, we encounter the Baroque style on every step within Prague. To name just a few: St Nicholas Church, the Loreto, Clementinum and most sculptures on Charles Bridge.

In mid-18th century, serious damages were caused to the city during the occupation by the French and Prussian armies, and the siege of the Prussians and the Austrians. In this turbulent period, the Austrian Empress Maria Theresa was crowned Czech Queen. Her reforms had a positive outcome not only for Prague but also for the entire country. In 1784, under the reign of her son Joseph II, the four cities of Prague were unified.

In terms of architecture, the Classical Baroque and Rococo are followed by Classicism by Historicism in the 2nd half of the 19th century. The unified city is growing, the first factories appear in the suburbs and the first railway arrived in the city. An example of planned construction of a new residential suburb from the early 19th century, is the core of present Karlin district. In addition to industrial buildings, a number of cultural buildings were built simultaneously, such as the National Museum and National Theatre in Neo-Renaissance style.

At the turn of the 20th century, Art Nouveau architecture ruled Prague and buildings in this style, such as the Municipal House, appeared in the centre.

After World War I and the collapse of the Austro-Hungarian Empire in 1918, the Czechoslovak Republic was proclaimed. In 1922, Great Prague was established, incorporating its suburban communities. In the 1930s, new residential areas with villas emerged in the suburbs. During World War II, the industrial suburbs were damaged, but the city centre was preserved almost untouched, despite a few damages caused to some buildings including the Old Town Hall.

In the 2nd half of the 20th centre, the city's architecture was marked by the Communist dictatorship. In the 1950s Socialist Realism dominated in architecture which is represented in Prague by the former Hotel International. The city was surrounded by housing estates. In 1974 the first metro line was opened.

After the Velvet Revolution (1989), architecturally interesting buildings appeared in Prague, such as the Dancing Building, the Golden Angel, the Danube House, the National Technical Library and the Main Point.

Petrin Hill is located near Prague Castle, above Lesser Town. The name derives from a Latin word "petra" i.e. "stone", perhaps due to the marlstone that was mined here between the Romanesque and Gothic periods to build the local buildings. The hill was originally covered by forest, replaced by vineyards in between 12th and early 16th century, their traces are visible to this date. Petrin Hill was divided by city walls called Hanger Wall during the reign of Charles IV in the 14th century. Massive bastions were added to the western part of the Wall during the Baroque period. The original Romanesque chapel (1135) on top of the hill was replaced by the Baroque Church of St Lawrence in 1770, today used by the Old Catholic Church.

On the occasion of the Jubilee Exhibition held in 1891, a mirror labyrinth and a 60m high tower were constructed at the top of the hill. Subsequently, the observatory (1928), rose garden (1930) and alpinium (1930) i.e. alpine garden were constructed. During the Exhibition, a funicular operated by a water counterbalancing system was used at Petrin Hill. The current (third) version of the funicular was constructed in 1985.

On the south side, there are two places worth visiting. The Empire style Kinsky Summer Palace (1827–1831) situated in Kinsky Garden, today used as Ethnographic Museum. And the wooden Church of St Michael donated to Prague by Carpathian Ruthenia in 1929, at the time part of the First Czechoslovak Republic. One can enjoy beautiful city scenes and admire countless statues on a walk around Petrin Hill. In springtime, the Hill is covered by fully blossoming lilacs and forsythias (colloquially called "golden rain"). In winter, locals use the slopes of the hill for sledding.

▲ *The Petrin Lookout Tower*

The Church of St Lawrence at Petrin Hill ▶

The Royal Canonry of Premonstratensians at Strahov is one of the oldest monasteries of the order in the world. It was founded by King Vladislav II and Bishop Jindrich Zdik in 1140 and it started functioning in 1143. Its position was of great strategic importance, as it was constructed at the foot of Petrin Hill, on Prague Castle's access road. A Baroque library can be found in the monastery which includes the famous Theological Hall (1671–1679) as well as the Philosophical Hall (1782–1784). The library accumulated over 200 000 books, including the most valuable volume Strahov Gospel (860–865) from the city of Trier. In 1627 the Church of Assumption of Virgin Mary, later nominated as a basilica by Pope John Paul II, received the body of St Norbert transferred from Magdeburg, Germany. He was the founder of the order.

▲ *The Church of St Roch at Strahov*

▲ *The entrance gate of Strahov Monastery*

The Church of the Assumption of the Virgin Mary at Strahov ▶

Strahov Library – the Philosophical Hall

Strahov Library – the Theological Hall

◀ *Church of the Assumption of the Virgin Mary*

Replicas of precious prints in Strahov library

After the Battle at White Mountain in 1620, foreign nobility arrived in and the cult of Our Lady of Loreto with them. After seeing the Chapel of Our Lady of Loreto in Mikulov, Baroness Benigna Lobkowitz decided to establish one in Prague. The chapel was built as a copy of the Holy House in the Italian city of Loreto. The Renaissance chapel with its rich stucco decoration is a work of Italian constructors. It is believed to be a precise copy of the Italian original including a few beams and bricks from the Italian Loreto used in its construction.

Later on, a Baroque arched hallway was built around the chapel, as well as the Church of the Birth of Our Lord (1734–1737) of the Capuchin Convent. The second most important treasury in the country, after the one of St Vitus Cathedral, is located on the first floor of the arched hallway. The most valuable object of the treasury is the late 17th century Diamond Monstrance, also called "Prague Sun", decorated with 6222 diamonds.

The 27 bells of carillon in the tower of the monastery play a melody for Virgin Mary every hour from 1694.

▲ *The carillon*

▲ *Loreto*

The interior of the Church of the Nativity of Our Lord ▶

▲ *The Holy House*

◀ *The Great Pearl monstrance*

▲ *The Wallenstein monstrance*

▲ *The Diamond monstrance (Prague Sun)*

▲ *The Lobkowicz monstrance*

The Ring monstrance ▲

Behind the oldest Bohemian Capuchin monastery and the Church of Our Lady Queen of the Angels, is an area called New World. After the 14th-century expansion of the city walls, the original small houses of the poor were squeezed in the corner of the walls. This area was repeatedly damaged by wars and fires and consequently rebuilt. This picturesque corner under the Baroque bastions is a place where time seems to have stopped and the hustle and bustle of the city does not reach to this day. New World retains its genius loci despite recent building reconstructions. Tycho Brahe briefly lived here and then died in 1601. Every day, believers from all over the world arrive in Prague for a pilgrimage to the Infant Jesus, including Pope Benedict XVI in 2009.

▲ *The Church of Our Lady Queen of Angels*

New World in Prague's Castle District ▲

The then town to the west of Prague Castle, this area is now called Hradcany Square, became fully subjected to the king in the 14th century. Other buildings already existed further away to the west, including the Brevnov and Strahov monasteries. The western side of Prague Castle was easily accessible and it was the most vulnerable in times of war. Therefore, Castle District (Hradcany) was surrounded by walls already during the reign of Charles IV in the 14th century. The city was damaged by wars and fires such as the fires during the Hussite Wars in 1420 and the great fire of Prague Castle and Lesser Town in 1541. The fire of 1541 was followed by Renaissance reconstruction and new construction of buildings. The best preserved Renaissance buildings are the Schwarzenberg Palace, the Martinic Palace and the Castle District Town Hall. Castle District became a royal town in 1598, under the rule of Rudolf II. The relocation of the imperial court from Vienna to Prague caused an influx of new residents and social differences. These are still apparent if you

▲ *The Cernin Palace*

A lamp-post in Loretanska ▶

▲ *The lower part of Hradcany Square with the Archbishopric Palace on the left and the main gate of the Castle in the background*

The upper part of Hradcany Square with the Church of St Benedict and Tuscany Palace ▲

The Schwarzenberg Palace, the plague column ▲

find yourself few steps from the Baroque palaces in the enclave of New Town.

After the defeat of the Czech Estates at White Mountain in 1620, the Swedish occupation and the pillaging in 1648, the majority of the buildings in Castle District were constructed by the Church, and the local and foreign nobility enriched by confiscations. The original Renaissance-style Holy House was used to create a foundation of the Baroque monastery, Loreto. In 1741, a part of the district was destroyed by the invasion of French and Bavarian troops and in the following year by fire. From the 17th century until the early 19th century, Castle District gradually became an area of monumental palaces and monasteries. In 1756, during the reign of Maria Theresa, Castle District was elevated to be the fourth town of Prague. However, in 1784 all four towns were united under a single municipal administration and gave birth to the city of Prague.

At the beginning of the 19th century, the Classical Salmov Palace was built next to the Castle. However, after the stagnation in construction work during the Napoleonic Wars, the economic strength of the nascent bourgeoisie was directed towards the development of new industrial suburbs. Thus, in terms of architecture, the structural development of Castle District was almost completed. In the 1960s gas lighting was introduced to the streets of Castle district. One of the original lampposts from 1867–1868 can be still seen in Hradcany Square by the Castle entrance. In the early 21st century, the Schwarzenberg and Salmov Palaces were modified for exhibition purposes of the National Gallery.

▲ *A beautiful view of Lesser Town and the Church of St Nicholas from Hradcany Square*

PRAGUE CASTLE

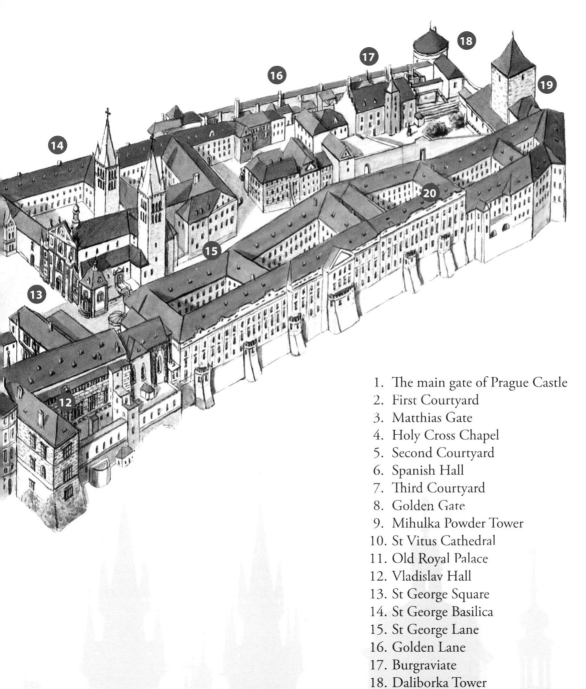

1. The main gate of Prague Castle
2. First Courtyard
3. Matthias Gate
4. Holy Cross Chapel
5. Second Courtyard
6. Spanish Hall
7. Third Courtyard
8. Golden Gate
9. Mihulka Powder Tower
10. St Vitus Cathedral
11. Old Royal Palace
12. Vladislav Hall
13. St George Square
14. St George Basilica
15. St George Lane
16. Golden Lane
17. Burgraviate
18. Daliborka Tower
19. Black Tower
20. Lobkowicz Palace

Prince Borivoj chose this location for building the ruler's residence for its strategic position, protected by the Vltava River on one side and by the Brusnice creek on another side. Thus, the seat of Premyslid dynasty was moved from Levy Hradek (10 kilometers north) to Prague Castle. The new seat, which was then more of a fortress than a castle, later became the centre of the newly founded feudal state. In the 2nd half of the 9th century, Prince Borivoj and his wife Princess Ludmila, later proclaimed a saint, were baptised by St Methodius in Velehrad in Great Moravia. Consequently, Borivoj founded the first Christian church at the Prague Castle., dedicated to Virgin Mary. Its foundations have been preserved to this day. This period represents not only the earliest history of the state but also the beginning of the city's continuous construction development.

Initially, Prague Castle was a fort with ramparts, earthworks, palisades and half-timbered stone buildings. The still existing Romanesque Basilica of St George, founded in 920, was the second church of Prague Castle and first monastery of Benedictine sisters. Around 923, the Romanesque St Vitus Rotunda was founded a, in which St Wenceslas, the Patron Saint of Bohemia, was buried in 929 or 935. In 973 a bishopric was established. In the mid-11th century, the earthen fortifications were replaced

▲ The banner of the President of the Republic

The Bastion Garden, renovated by Josip Plecnik ▲
The main entrance of Prague Castle with the large statues of fighting giants, Matthias's Gate in the background ▶

⑫

by stone ones ,and in the mid-12th century i.e. the reign of Sobeslav I, a stone princely palace was constructed. In the 13th and early 14th century, under the rule of King Přemysl Otakar II and King Wenceslas II, the buildings of the castle were enlarged and its fortifications were strengthened. After Přemysl Otakar II consolidated his political power and Wenceslas II strengthened his economical power by introducing the silver Prague Groschen,

the castle and its surrounding area expanded. Wenceslas II strove to unite the Czech lands and Poland, and became King of Czech as well as King of Poland. Under the reign of Wenceslas II the Premyslid realm was temporary larger than the Holy Roman Empire. Wenceslas II helped his son to obtain the Hungarian crown, thus becoming a king at the age of 12. He was murdered five years later (1306) in Olomouc as the last male heir of Premyslid, which caused

the dynasty to die out. At the same time, the castle's Romanesque phase ended.

After a brief interregnum the throne was offered to John of Luxembourg in 1309. He became King of Bohemia following the marriage with Elizabeth of Premyslid dynasty. After long disputes with the local nobility, King John left Bohemia and returned only sporadically. The king's long absence led to a gradual weakening of royal power and strengthening of the position

◀ *The Baroque Kohl's (also Lions' or Leopold's) fountain in the second courtyard of Prague Castle*　　　*The Spanish Hall* ▲

of nobility, and thus the country was on the brink of war. The son of the royal couple, who later became the Emperor and King Charles IV, was brought up his uncle, the King of France. When young Prince Charles arrived in Prague in 1333, the Castle was so devastated that he had to reside in Old Town. The efforts of some nobles to create friction between King John and his son were unsuccessful. While King John was still alive, the Pope elevated Prague bishopric to an archbishopric, which could be credited to Charles. This was an official impulse for King John and Prince Charles to establish the Sts Vitus, Wenceslas and Adalbert Cathedral at Prague Castle in 1344. In this way, a new style arrived in Bohemia directly from France, the High Gothic. Charles summoned a French architect, Matthias of Arras, to direct the construction until his death in 1352. His successor, Peter Parler of Cologne

▲ *The facade of St Vitus, St Wenceslas and St Adalbert Cathedral*

St Vitus Cathedral, the third courtyard with the granite obelisk ▶

completed the apse chapel and the vaults, and began the construction of St Wenceslas Chapel, the main tower and the Golden Gate. During this period Prague Castle underwent major changes. In order to free space for the cathedral, an older Romanesque basilica was demolished, a new wing of the Royal Palace was built and the castle fortifications were reconstructed. Charles IV was crowned King of Bohemia. The following period (1348–1357) was not only the peak of the diplomatic activity of Charles IV, but also an important milestone for

the city. In 1348 Charles IV established a university and New Town of Prague in 1348, and a stone bridge, now called Charles Bridge, in 1357. This golden era was completed by his coronation as Holy Roman Emperor of Bohemia and as emperor in Rome. Prague became an important metropolis of the kingdom and the empire. After the death of Charles IV, during the reign of his son Wenceslas IV, the decline of the city was further aggravated by the Black Death, economic recession and indecisiveness of the King. At this time

vicar-general John of Nepomuk, who was later canonised, died after being tortured. A period of social unrest called, called the Hussite Wars, broke out fully in 1419, the year of the King's death.

In the 15th century, the significance of the Castle as the king's residence declined. The Hussites viewed it only as a stronghold of their opponent, King Wenceslas IV's brother, Emperor and King Sigismund of Luxembourg. Prague Castle is conquered by the Hussites, then acquired back, and lost again when Emperor Sigismund fled Bohe-

▲ *Mosaic depicting the Last Judgement*

The east side of the cathedral, St George Square ▶

mia and the Castle Guard surrendered. During the Hussite Wars the cathedral and other buildings of the Castle and the Castle District were damaged, burnt out and burglarized. In 1421, the Mayor of Prague took over the Castle. In 1458, George of Podebrady was elected King of Bohemia in the Old Town Hall. The Castle was so ravaged that the kings had to reside in King's Court in Old Town.

The constructions at the Castle were revived again at the end of the 15th century, during the reign of King Wladyslaw II Jagiello, who decided to relocate from King's Court to the Castle. The Late Gothic style is preserved by the Royal Oratory in the cathedral and the vaulted space of the Royal Palace. However, architect Benedikt Ried started using Renaissance elements in the Royal Palace. The Gothic vaults were combined with Renaissance windows and overdoors in Vladislav Hall (1490–1502). A new wing of the Royal Palace was built on the south side and the castle fortifications were strengthened on the north side. After the end of the Jagiello dynasty, Ferdinand of Habsburg took the throne in 1526. Thus, the Renaissance style started to flourish in Prague, boosted by the arrival of Italian builders and craftsmen. A representative building of this style was the Queen Anne's Summer Palace in the newly founded Royal Gardens of Prague Castle, also called Belvedere. Its construction began in 1538 and the gardens were decorated with the Singing Fountain in 1562. Nevertheless, the construction of the summer palace was interrupted by the great fire of 1541 and subsequently by the Black Death. The fire damaged the Old Royal Palace and the Royal All Saints Chapel and completely burnt out the royal library. After the fire in the late 16th

◀ *The interior of the cathedral*

The tomb of St John of Nepomuk ▲

▲ *Mucha's window in St Vitus Cathedral*

▲ *St Wenceslas Chapel*

century, the Castle was repaired and new buildings were constructed such as the Rosenberg and Lobkowicz Palaces, the new Burgraviate and the castle gates and fortifications. The main tower of the cathedral was equipped with a new Renaissance dome. In 1583, Emperor Rudolf II moved with his court to Prague. The already old Royal Palace did not fulfil the demands of the emperor and so he had new buildings constructed on the western and northern sides of the Castle and in the Royal Gardens. The Royal Mausoleum and the new Royal Tomb were built inside the cathedral. In 1597, Rudolf II allowed the castle marksmen to build small houses in the space under the arches of the northern wall of the Castle, thus giving birth to the Golden Lane. The imperial court was full of artists, scientists and charlatans. The Emperor, being a passionate collector of paintings, sculptures and curiosities, constructed new premises in the Castle to house his many collections. Rudolph II was forced to abdicate in 1611 and was succeeded by his brother Emperor Matthias. The entrance of Prague Castle so called Matthias Gate serves as a reminder of the Emperor's reign. This originally triumphal free-standing arch was the first and therefore the oldest Baroque structure in Prague. However, it was later incorporated into the surrounding Neo-Classical buildings.

The revolt of Bohemian estates and defenestration of the imperial governors at Prague Castle in 1618 were early signs of the upcoming Thirty Years' War. The elected king Frederick V Elector Palatine fled the country after less than seven months in power. The Bohemian estates' troops were defeated in the Battle of White Mountain in 1620 and the leaders of the rebellion were executed the following year at Old Town Square. During the war, the Castle was conquered and occupied by the Saxons (1631–1632) . In 1648, the Castle, Castle District and Lesser Town were pillaged by the Swedish. This experience led to the strengthening of the fortifications of the Castle and the whole city. The buildings of the third courtyard were unified, the line of buildings between the second and third courtyard was completed, chapels and fountains were built , and the already existing buildings were redesigned. In 1673, during the reign of Emperor Leopold I, the constructions of the Cathedral of St Vitus restarted again but were interrupt by the war with Ottoman Empire. The importance of the Castle declined. In 1723, the celebration of the coronation of Emperor Charles VI as King of Bohemia taking place at the Castle was a reminder of its glorious times. The celebrations of the beatification and canonization of St John of Nepomuk in the subsequent years added to the glory. A chapel dedicated to this saint was added to St George's Basilica and a monumental tomb made of silver was placed in the cathedral in his honor (1733–1736). However, the Castle's constricted space did not favour the construction of monumental Baroque palaces and churches. In the 18th c., Prague was repeatedly conquered and plundered by foreign armies – the French, Saxons and Bavarians in 1741, and the Prussians in 1744. Empress Maria Theresa ordered the reconstruction of the entire western wing of the Castle, from Old Royal Palace to Rudolph Gallery (1755–1775). The Vien-

continue on page 48

The tomb of St John of Nepomuk ▲

Above the southern Golden Gate of the St Vitus, St Wenceslas and St Adalbert Cathedral, in a small chamber not accessible to the public, the Czech Crown Jewels are kept behind a door locked with seven locks. The seven keys are in the possession of seven key holders: the President, the Prime Minister, the Archbishop of Prague, the President of the Senate, the President of the Chamber of Deputies, the Dean of the Metropolitan Chapter of St Vitus Cathedral and the Mayor of Prague.

The Crown Jewels consist of a crown, orb, sceptre, robes, case for the crown, crown cushions, cases for the orb and cases for the scepter.

The Royal Crown dedicated to St Wenceslas

The original crown of the Premyslid dynasty was not preserved. Its image is found only on coins and preserved burial royal insignia. The so-called Czech Crown disappeared after the coronation of Beatrix of Bourbon, the wife of King John of Luxembourg, in the early 14th century.

The son of King John, Charles IV, ordered the making of a new crown and other crown jewels in 1346, while he was still Margrave of Moravia. The crown was dedicated to St Wenceslas and placed in the saint's chapel in the cathedral on order of Charles IV. Kings were to use it only on the day of their coronation. It is usually depicted with a red bishop's mitre which was allowed to be used even by some Premyslid princes.

The crown visually follows the Premyslid crowns but its lilies resemble the crowns of French kings. The crown is made of 19, 20 and 22 karat gold.

At the top of the crown there is a cross with a thorn from Christ's crown, probably from Romanesque period. The crown is decorated with pearls and 96 precious stones, the two largest of which are a big red rubelite and a nearly 300 carat blue sapphire.

In 1347, when Charles IV was both King of Bohemia as well as King of the Romans, he had a case made for the crown, which became part of the Crown Jewels.

The Royal Orb and Royal Sceptre

The orb and the sceptre made of 18 karat gold and decorated with precious stones and pearls were made in the early 16th century for King Ferdinand I of Habsburg. The case for the sceptre probably dates from the 17th century. On the occasion of St Wenceslas' millennium in 1929, the Crown Jewels were exhibited and the damaged case of the orb was replaced by a new one. The original orb and sceptre, which Charles IV had made for his coronation as King of the Romans, are now probably kept in Vienna at the Imperial Treasury at Hofburg Palace.

Items used for coronations but stored in places other than the chamber

The silk and ermine coronation robe that was made for the coronation of Ferdinand II in 1617, is now stored in an air-conditioned depositary at Prague Castle.

The coronation cross and the sword of St Wenceslas, probably from the 13th century, are part of the St Vitus treasure and were never kept in the chamber with the Crown Jewels.

The Crown Jewels are exhibited only for a short period of time on special occasions and anniversaries.

The Royal Orb

The Royal Scepter ▲   ▲ *The Crown of St Wenceslas*

continued from page 45
nese architect Nicolo Pacassi unified the diverse buildings under a common façade. Thus, the Castle's courtyard gained a design similar to other Picassi's buildings in Vienna and Budapest. A new first courtyard was constructed, so-called Courtyard of Honour. The Chapel of the Holy Cross designed by Anselmo Lurago was built in the second courtyard in 1756, and the Institute for Noble Women (1754–1755) designed by Pacassi was established in the third courtyard.

During the rule of Joseph II, the Castle lost its importance as a royal residence. Its many parts were completely abandoned and it were used as army barracks. In the first half of the 19th Big changes in the overall layout of the cCastle arrived in the second half of the 19th century. After the revolution in 1848, a brick wall was erected on the southern side of the gardens. Between 1865 and 1868, the Spanish Hall and the New Hall were reconstructed due to the intended coronation of Emperor

Francis Joseph I. In 1873 the foundation stone for the completion of the cathedral was laid. Space for the new construction was necessary and so St Adalbert's Chapel was demolished and other buildings were modified. The Czechoslovak Republic was proclaimed after the World War I in 1918. Other major modifications to the overall layout of the Castle were made by the Slovenian architect Josip Plecnik. Some interiors were renovated and the area around the cathedral was reconstructed. Plecnik's

▲ The Old Royal Palace

Vladislav Hall ▶

▲ St George Basilica

St George's Basilica, the tomb of Prince Vratislav I. ▲

work at the southern gardens gave the Castle extra monumentality suitable for the seat of the President. A granite obelisk was placed in the third courtyard in 1928 to celebrate the tenth anniversary of the Republic and to commemorate the victims of World War I. In 1929, on the occasion of St Wenceslas millennium, the finished cathedral was opened. The presidential shelters still inaccessible to this day create an interesting topic. The first one was air-raid shelter constructed in 1938 was used by President Hacha during the Nazi occupation. After the communist coup, President Zapotocky had a secret nuclear shelter built in 1958, located in the third courtyard. Repairs and renovations followed the World War II. In the 1960s, an extensive archaeological research took place and some spaces were adjusted for reception and exhibition purposes. After the Velvet Revolution in 1989, more parts of Prague Castle became open to the public. The Royal Gardens with its newly opened Orangery as well as the Stag Moat became accessible to all. An underpass was built beneath the Powder Bridge and the residence of the president was transferred from the Royal Gardens to the renovated Classicist Lumbe Villa at the beginning of the Stag Moat.

◀ *The Golden Lane, Franz Kafka's house*

Queen Anne's Summer Palace (Belvedere), the Singing Fountain ▲

▲ *Gardens of Prague Castle*

The early settlement of present Lesser Town consisted of scattered buildings. The first buildings around the market place under the Castle appeared soon after its foundation. The position of this settlement was favourable also due to sufficient water supply from Petrin Hill. Several buildings and a wooden bridge were already mentioned in the 12th century. The existence of a bridge over the river is supported by historical records. According to one report the body of murdered Prince Wenceslas was taken over the bridge in the 930s and a later report mentions a flood in 1118, when the water rose above the bridge. Religious buildings already existed as well, such as Romanesque churches in the centre of the scattered set-

▲ *The House at the Two Suns where writer Jan Neruda lived in 1845-57*

Nerudova Street with Strahov Monastery in the background ▲

▲ *Nerudova Street, house emblems on the right*

(18)

▲ *The Church of St Nicholas in Lesser Town*

tlements, the Bishop's Court and the Johannite monastery with its Romanesque Church of Virgin Mary under the Chain. Only fragments of the Romanesque-style settlement have been preserved.

Development of trade on both banks of Vltava River led King Vladislav, c. 1170, to establish the first stone bridge in Prague, which was named after his wife Queen Judith. We do not know the exact date of the foundation of the bridge nor the name of the Italian architect who built it. The connection of the two riverbanks by Judith Bridge led to stronger building development in Lesser Town. However, compare to Old Town Lesser Town was smaller and so it was called Smaller Town of Prague.

In the 13th century, new order was bestowed upon the existing spontaneous and disorganised settlement under the Castle. In 1253, part of the settlement was surrounded by walls and in 1257 King Ottokar II founded a royal city in this area. He then expelled most of the Czech population and invited German colonists. A large square was created in the middle of the new city and the already existing Romanesque Church of St Wenceslas was preserved in the centre of the square. At the end of the 13th century,, this church was already too small and so the larger Gothic church of St Nicholas was built in its vicinity in 1283. The size of the square was approximately the same as the size of the main square of Lesser Town, in the centre of which now stands the Baroque Church of St Nicholas. The St Wenceslas Church was taler replaced by a Jesuit collage.

Under the reign of John of Luxembourg and Charles IV, Lesser Town expanded significantly towards south. Important fortifications were constructed as well as Gothic buildings along the main roads, facing the street. In 1342 Judith Bridge was destroyed by floods and soon after, in 1357, Charles IV initiated the construction of present Charles Bridge. In the Augustinian monastery of St Thomas, first brewery of Prague was established in 1358. In 1360, Charles IV began the construction of new walls e, thus, enlarging the fortified area of Lesser Town. The Romanesque Archbishopric Court was rebuilt in Gothic style and its Gothic tower has been preserved to this day. The Johannites replaced the Romanesque Basilica of Virgin Mary under the Chain with a new Gothic church with the same name. After the death of Charles IV, during the reign of Wenceslas IV, times of economic decline and growing social crisis followed. The seat of the Archbishop along with the rich monasteries of Lesser Town formed a counterweight to the Royal Castle. The disputes between King Wenceslas IV and the Archbishop culminated in 1393 with the arrest and subsequent torture and death of Vicar General John of Nepomuk, whose body was later thrown over the Charles Bridge into Vltava River. After the death of Wenceslas IV in 1419, the social crisis culminated in a rebellion. After the defenestration of New Town councillor from the New Town Hall, the rebellious

The interior of St Nicholas Church ▲

(19)

▲ *Wallenstein Garden*

Hussite troops crossed Charles Bridge and through Lesser Town headed towards the Castle. Lesser Town was repeatedly burned and several houses and monasteries were damaged and pillaged. Lesser Town started recovering very slowly and only after the Hussite Wars, during the reign of King George of Podebrady, in the 2nd half of the 15th century, more intense building development began. After 1485, when King Vladislav II Jagiello permanently moved back to the Castle, many courtiers started constructing their palaces in Lesser Town. Gothic-style revival of the town was stopped by a fire in 1503. However, dozens of houses were restored relatively quickly in Late Gothic style. The great fire of 1541 was devastating for almost two-thirds of the houses in Lesser Town. After 1550, the recovery of the city became even more difficult because of the recurring Black Death epidemics.

In 1575 Rudolf II of Habsburg was crowned Czech King and he moved the Imperial Court from Vienna to Prague. Builders, artists, scholars and scientists like Tycho Brahe and Johannes Kepler, merchants but also charlatans and adventurers arrived in Prague. In 1583–1612 Prague was gradually turned into a cosmopolitan city. The Imperial Court was the seat of permanent foreign ambassadors and it was visited by delegations of monarchs from distant

Wallenstein Garden ▲

lands, such as the Shah of Persia and Russian Tsar Fjodor Ivanovic. The glory of the Imperial Court led to new construction and reconstruction in Renaissance style in Lesser Town. Wealthy Italians founded an Italian congregational community in the Chapel of the Assumption of Virgin Mary in Lesser Town and an Italian hospital under Petrin Hill (1609). Thanks to religious tolerance, German Lutherans founded the Holy Trinity Church, the first Baroque church in Prague, in 1611. It was given to the Barefoot Carmelites after the Battle of White Mountain, was dedicated to Our Lady Victorious and made famous worldwide by Infant Jesus. The emperor was indecisive in regards to religious matters. After arriving in Prague he did not promote aggressive catholicization due to the financial dependence on the Czech non-Catholic Estates. In addition, the emperor was ill and he was not addressing the growing problems. Therefore, the opposing groups were fighting for power in the political arena. The issuing of the Imperial Letter of Majesty in 1609, confirming religious freedom, came too late. The troops of Bishop of Passau Leopold von Habsburg arrived in Prague to restore the waning political power of the emperor but instead they pillaged Lesser Town in 1611. Rudolf II was forced to abdicate and his brother Matthias, a supporter of re-catholicization,

21

▲ *The Vrtba Garden with St Vitus Cathedral in the background*

became emperor. The first Early Baroque style buildings were erected in Lesser Town, such as the Church of St Charles Borromeo at the Italian hospital. The religious disputes culminated after the defenestration of the imperial governors at the Castle in 1618.

The Protestant "Winter King" Frederick V Elector Palatine was crowned Czech King in 1619 and fled the country soon after. In 1620 the Czech Estates were defeated in the Battle of White Mountain. In 1621 the leaders of the uprising were executed. The 1622 general pardon had no effect on the confiscations and fines imposed upon the Czech Estates. Generals, military commanders, foreign nobility and the Catholic Church benefited from the victory at White Mountain. The victors soon started transforming Lesser Town. The largest and most magnificent Early Baroque-style palace competed with its pomp with Prague Castle and was built in Lesser Town by one of the military leaders, Albrecht von Wallenstein, who later became duke and was appointed Imperial Generalissimo. Palaces were renovated in Baroque style and new Baroque palaces and gardens were created. Unfortunately, the Thirty Years' War did not leave Prague untouched. Prague was occupied by the Saxons from 1631 to 1632. The Swedish army occupied and pillaged the left bank in 1648. The efforts of the Swedish to reach the right bank by crossing Charles Bridge were deterred and they left Prague with their loot after the Peace of Westphalia in 1649. The Thirty Years' War and the subsequent post-war period led to the construction of Baroque fortifica-

tions of Prague Castle and Lesser Town, which was completed in 1721. The most beautiful Baroque building in Prague, St Nicholas Church in the middle of Lesser Town Square, was constructed by the Jesuits (1704–1755). In the 18th century, Baroque renovations and new buildings gave Lesser Town its current look and Charles Bridge was decorated with Baroque statues of saints. In 1784 Emperor Joseph II issued a decree for the merger of the four towns of Prague.

The beginning of the 19th century, was marked by the development of trade and industry, and the centre of activity shifted to the right bank. Empire and Biedermeier, the new fashionable styles, also arrived in Lesser Town but noticeably influenced only its outskirts. Empire style townhouses were erected in the southern part, and a new road leading to the Castle was constructed in the northern part. In the mid-19th century, the territory of Lesser Town was defined as the space between the chain bridge (now Legion Bridge) in the south and the chain footbridge in the north. The remaining available land within this space was used for new buildings. A hospital, church and teachers' house were constructed on the slopes of Petrin Hill. At the riverbank, mill houses were enlarged and a brickyard was established. In 1890, Charles Bridge was badly damaged by a flood. One arch and two sculptures collapsed into the river but since the bridge was an important part of the city's communication, it was repaired within two years.

At the end of the 19th century, parts of the fortifications of Lesser Town started disappearing the Ujezd Gate (1892) and several houses in the southern part of the Lesser Square (1896) were demolished, which cleared space for traffic to pass through Lesser Town. However, the lifestyle of people in Lesser Town had not changed much compared to other parts of Prague. The atmosphere was captured by Jan Neruda in his "Lesser Town Tales". This poet and writer lived in Lesser Town in the house called At the Two Suns situated on the street that now bears his name.

At the turn of the situated on the 20th century, the traffic in Lesser Town increased. In the years 1905–1908 public buses begin to run over Charles Bridge. However, the bus line connecting Lesser Town with Prague Castle, running through Nerudova Street, launched in 1908, did not last for long. It was cancelled one and a half year later after (1909) a serious accident. At the same time a tram line started running through Lesser Town. Another tram with ground-level power supply was running even over Charles Bridge up until 1908.

After World War I and the proclamation of the Czechoslovak Republic, some of Lesser Town's palaces were turned into offices and institutions and others started to serve as embassies. In the period between the two world wars, only a few buildings were demolished or built. World War II did not cause serious damage to Lesser Town either. It wasn't until the 1970s when, due to traffic demands, some adjustments were made. In 1968 the construction of metro line A began and Malostranska station was opened in 1978 at the periphery of Lesser Town.

After the fall of Communist regime in 1989, the façades of some palaces were renovated and their use changed. The Wallenstein Palace became the seat of the Senate and the Liechtenstein Palace was modified for official receptions of the government. In 2002 parts of Lesser Town and the metro were flooded. After the restorations, a mobile anti-flood barrier system was installed for protection.

Today's Lesser Town is a lively district and popular tourist destination with many cafés, restaurants, hotels, shops, small museums and galleries.

St Nicholas Church with Petrin Hill in the background ▲

KAMPA ISLAND

This floodplain on the bank of the River Vltava remained undeveloped for a long time. In order to power up the newly emerging mill houses in the 14th century, a man-made canal, today called Certovka, was built and separated Kampa from Lesser Town. A segment of this canal near Charles Bridge is called Prague Venice.

The two mill wheels located in Certovka are newly renovated and so is the Renaissance Grand Priory Mill from the 16th century. There is a small enclave, beside Charles Bridge, of houses, some of which date from the early 17th century. The largest of the palaces of Kampa Island, the Liechtenstein Palace, is used by the government for official receptions.

A staircase leading from Charles Bridge was built in 1884, which made Kampa Island easily accessible. The Kampa Museum, formal Sova's Mills, is located in Baroque gardens which are now used as a public park. The original mills had to been reconstructed to house the museum's unique collection of modern art.

Kampa Island with Certovka watermill canal ▲

Infant Jesus has been worshiped all around the world. A tangible worldwide expression of the worship is Infant Jesus of Prague. The statue of Infant Jesus of Prague comes from Andalusia, where according to legend, a monk brother Joseph modelled it in wax after the Infant Jesus appeared to him. The statue was brought to Prague in 1556 by a Spanish noblewoman Maria Manrique de Lara y Mendoza, a lady-in-waiting of the future Empress Maria of Spain. She had received the Infant Jesus statue as a wedding gift for her wedding to the Supreme Chancellor of Bohemian Kingdom Vratislav II of Pernstein. In 1628, their daughter Polyxena donated this family heirloom to Discalced Carmelites at the Church of Our Lady Victorious. The statue was damaged by Protestants (1631) and was later repaired by Cyril's father, who is also the author of the best-known prayer to Infant Jesus. In the following period, the vestments of the Infant Jesus statue were changed according to the religious calendar, i.e. white for Christmas and Easter, red for the Holy Spirit festivities, purple during Advent, gold on other festive occasions and green in the interim. The most important was a green vestment with gold embroidery, hand-embroidered by Empress Maria Theresa. Believers bring vestments as gifts to Infant Jesus to this day. In 1996, the Manrique de Lara family gave Infant Jesus a vestment sewn from ancient priestly garments. Some of the most valuable vestments can be seen in the museum of the church. On the occasion of the world exhibition Expo 92, a copy of Infant Jesus of Prague was donated to the Basilica of Santa Maria de la Esperanza Macarena in Seville in May 1992. After the Velvet Revolution, President Vaclav Havel, made a state visit to Chile, during which gave a copy of Infant Jesus of Prague to a church on Easter Island. Italian Carmelite fathers established a provincial delegation of Ligurian province of the Order in Prague to provide support to foreign missionaries in the Central African Republic.

Every day, believers from all over the world arrive in Prague for a pilgrimage to the Infant Jesus, including Pope Benedict XVI in 2009.

23

A wooden bridge over Vltava River where Charles Bridge stands today, is first mentioned in a report from 929, stating its destruction by floods. After the last of the wooden bridges was destroyed by floods in 1157, King Vladislav II decided to have a stone bridge constructed instead. The bridge was allegedly built in only two years and it was named Judith Bridge after the King's wife. This bridge was also destroyed by floods in 1342.

In 1357 Charles IV founded a bigger, more massive stone bridge, the present Charles Bridge. Various legends and theories emerged, regarding the foundation and construction of the bridge. The best-known legend, about constructors adding egg in the binder, was proven false after a chemical analysis. According to another popular theory, Charles IV laid the foundation stone of the bridge in 1357 on 9th July (7th month) at 5:31. The numbers 135797531 form a palindrome, a "magical number" which were meant to guarantee the endurance of the bridge. Nonetheless, the Charles Bridge was damaged by floods numerous times. In the 1432, 1784 and 1890, the damages were so severe that even some arches were destroyed. The bridge was also damaged in the 1st half of the 15th century during the Hussite Wars, in 1648 at the end of the Thirty Years' War and in June 1848 during the Pentecostal Uprising.

Thirty sculptures were placed on the bridge. The oldest and only bronze statue of St John of Nepomuk is from 1683. Some of the Baroque sculptures were replaced by Neo-Gothic ones after the bridge damage in 1890. The newest sculptural group is of Sts Cyril and Methodius from 1928–1938. Presently, some of the Baroque statues and sculptural groups are being replaced by copies and the bridge is being gradually reconstructed..

▲ *The statue of St Lutgarde on Charles Bridge*

CHARLES BRIDGE

(24)

Charles Bridge with the Lesser Town Bridge Towers ▲

▲ *Charles Bridge with the Lesser Town Bridge Towers*

St Wenceslas (c 907–929 or 935)

In the 10th century, Prince Wenceslas attempted to keep the Kingdom united by avoiding further warfare. After the defeat by the East Frankish Kingdom in 929, he agreed to start paying a "peace tax" to King Henry I, from whom he then received the relic of St Vitus and founded a rotunda at Prague Castle dedicated to him. Wenceslas' stance was criticised not only by his opponents but also by his brother Boleslav who arranged his murder in Stara Boleslav in 929 or 935. Three years later his body was taken to Prague Castle and buried in St Vitus Rotunda and later moved to St Wenceslas Chapel. Wenceslas was proclaimed a saint and then worshiped as a patron of Bohemia. He is usually depicted with a spear and a shield with a black eagle, the symbol of Premyslid dynasty. His most famous statue is in the centre of Prague, Wenceslas on a horse at the top of a square bearing his name.

The statue of St Wenceslas on Charles Bridge ▲

St John of Nepomuk (1345–1393)

At the end of the 14th century, Vicar General John of Nepomuk became a victim of a power dispute between King Wenceslas IV and Archbishop John of Jenstein. During one of the meetings in 1393, John of Nepomuk and three other members of the archbishop's escort were captured and tortured. However, only John of Nepomuk was never released and tortured to death. The reason was either the naming of a new abbot of the Kladruby Monastery by John of Nepomuk, of whom the King did not approve, or his refusal to divulge the confessions of Queen Sophia to the King. According to legend, the King himself took part in the torture. John's dead body was put in a sack and thrown into the river from Charles Bridge. It was pulled out by the Knights of the Cross and buried in the Church of the Holy Cross, in their convent. Soon after his death, he was recognised as a martyr. Around 1416, his body was transferred and buried inside St Vitus Cathedral. He was beatified in 1721 and canonised in 1729. In 1730, his relic was placed in a silver coffin in the middle of his Baroque tomb. More than two tons of silver were used in the making of the tomb.

The only bronze and oldest statue on Charles Bridge represents the saint holding a cross, symbolizing his refusal to divulge the secrets of the confessional. Two stone boards on the pedestal of the statue depict the legend of the confession and the throwing off the bridge. Another board on the bridge marks the point from which he was thrown into the river. According to a chronicle, whoever touches the latter board and makes a wish, would have their wish granted. The cult of St John of Nepomuk was spread by the Jesuits to Bavaria and Latin America.

▲ *The statue of St John of Nepomuk on Charles Bridge*

Charles Bridge, the Church of St Francis of Assisi on the left ▲

In the centre of Old Town lies Old Town Square, originally a marketplace surrounded by emerging settlements since the 10th century. The Romanesque Rotunda of the Holy Cross was built at the turn of the 12th century, (restored in 1864–1865). The town prospered because of trade and crafts. In the 12th century new stone buildings were built by both townspeople and the Church. King Wenceslas I founded the Franciscan Church of St James in 1232 and the, a monastery of St Agnes Convent of Poor Clares in 1234. The first abbess of the convent was the King's sister, St Agnes of Bohemia. Nonetheless, there were still spontaneous building sites emerging in Old Town. The population was diverse as well – Czechs, Germans, and Jewish merchants. In the 1230s Old Town became a municipality. At that time, a new marketplace was formed near Old Town Square, along with a small community surrounding it, called New Town by St Gall (Havel). It even had a status of an autonomous town within Old until 1287.

After many futile attempts to establish a town hall in Old Town, the permission was eventually given by King John of Luxembourg in 1338. The locals bought the house of merchant Wolfin of Kamen in the centre of Old Town for the premises of the town hall. A tower (1364) and more houses were successively added to the original building. Today, they form the complex of the Old Town Hall. As the first town

▲ *The statue of Charles IV*

A view of Krizovnicke Square from the Old Town Bridge Tower ▲

▲ *Rudolfinum*

▲ *Clementinum*

The Baroque hall of the library ▲

hall in the Kingdom, it confirmed the rise of the social status of the Old Town citizens. In 1348, Charles IV founded a university in Old Town. Due to the absence of any university premises, the classes were taking place in churches and professors' homes. It was not until 1386 that the university received its first building from King Wenceslas IV, today called Carolinum.

In the mid-14th century, guilds were formed. In 1348, New Town was established and thereafter united with Old Town on the royal order of Charles IV. Old Town citizens gained a dominant possition in the joint City Council (1367–1475). On the unification, the city walls of Old Town were demolished (their construction began under the rule of King Wenceslas I in the 13th century and was completed only around 1310). Old Town gained the right to participate in the control of common walls on the

▲ *Karlova Street*

some house emblems ▲

borders of New Town and also had the right to collect tax on Charles Bridge. The unification of Old Town and New Town led to the transformation of ethnic and social composition of the population. Based on orders of Charles IV some craftsmen had to move from the Old to New Town, while wealthier citizens remained in Old Town. The first report of the Old Town astronomical clock is from 1410.

The turn of the 15th century, was an era of economic decline and religious conflicts. The indecisiveness of King Wenseslas IV caused a pogrom against the Jewish population of Prague ghetto in 1389. King Wenceslas IV was a supporter of priest Jan Hus based in the newly established and private Bethlehem Chapel. Master Jan Hus became dean and later rector of Prague university and was preaching for the revival of Church in the Bethlehem Chaple. King Wenceslas IV struggled with the Church and the Noblemen's Union and he was even imprisoned several times The growing tension in both the academic and the social sphere was underlined by the Papal Schism and the rivalry between Wenceslas IV and Ruprecht II the Elector Palatine for the title of Holy Roman Emperor.

The Kutna Hora Decree, issued by King Wenceslas IV in 1409, changed the proportion of student votes in Charles University to the benefit of the Czechs against other nations. In protest, about 800 German students and professors left Prague for other universities, which led to the establishment of Leipzig University.

Master Jan Hus was excommunicated and Prague was placed under an interdict. continue on page 84

The Church of St Jilji (St Giles) in Old Town ▲

▲ *Old Town Square, Old Town Hall on the left, Tyn Church in the background*

The Astronomical Clock ▲

▲ St James the Less or son of Alphaeus

▲ St Andrew

▲ St Thaddaeus, also called Jude Thaddaeus or Jude of James

▲ St Thomas

▲ St John the Evangelist, son of Zebedee and the younger brother of James

▲ St Barnabas

▲ St Peter, originally named Simon

▲ St Matthew

▲ St Philip

▲ St Paul of Tarsus

▲ St Simon the Canaanite

▲ St Bartholomew

1. The rooster - an old symbol of courage and vigilance. It welcomes the new day and the sun. Its crow signals the end of the procession of the apostles.

2. The angel - the protector of the clock

3. The moving statuettes of the apostles.

4. Vanity - the statuette represents a man admiring his reflection in a mirror while moving

5. Avarice - during the procession of the apostles, the statuette shakes a pouch of money and is moving its cane. It symbolises avarice.

6. Old Bohemian time

7. Death - the statuette turns an hourglass counting the time of life and by pulling on a string it mournfully tolls a bell placed in a small tower above the clock.

8. The Turk - the statuette is considered to represent pleasures and vices.

9. The golden hand - the main pointer of the clock completes a full circle in 24 hours.

10. The hand pointing to sidereal time

11. The position of the Moon

12. The position of the Sun

13. Day

14. The ecliptic

15. The centre of the dial

16. Dawn

17. The zodiac

18. The tropic of Capricorn

19. The celestial equator

20. Night

21. The equator

22. Twilight

23. The astronomical dial

24. The tropic of Cancer

25. The philosopher, studying the world

26. Archangel Michael

27. The astronomer, studying the sky

28. The chronicler, recording events and history

29. The calendar by Josef Mánes

The astronomical clock dates back to 1410. It has undergone numerous changes over the centuries. At the end of World War II, during the Prague Uprising in May 1945, the clock was gravely damaged. The mechanism of the clock collapsed during a fire, the statues of the apostles were burned and both dials were damaged. After World War II, the clock was restored to its original form.

The clock is in the centre of the historical town on the right bank of Vltava River, and crowds of curious tourists stand in front of it to witness the march of the apostles, which happens every hour from morning to evening. A bell rings four times, the window opens and the apostles appear one after another, looking down at the crowd. At the same time the statues to the left and to the right of the upper dial are moving. We then hear crowing of a rooster while flapping its wings. Finally, the number of tolls of another bell indicates the hour.

The oldest part of the clock is an astronomical dial with a globe in its centre (see image on the next page). There is a golden hand on the hour hand moving on the dark exterior circle on the periphery of the whole dial, which shows the old Bohemian time i.e. the number of hours since the last sunset. Also, it points to the Roman numerals referring to civil time and to the Arabic numerals referring to Babylonian time, according to which the day is divided into 12 equal parts from sunrise to sunset. The gold circle, enclosing the coloured part of the dial, repre-

an approximate date. There sphere, representing the Moon, indicates not only the phase of the Moon but also its zodiacal constellation.

Below the astronomical dial (see image on the previous page). is the calendar dial. The original dial, from 1659, was replaced in 1865 by a new one which was replaced in 1880 by a copy destroyed at the end of World War II and then again replaced by yet another copy. The original one from 1865 is located in Prague City Museum.

The calendar dial completes one rotation per year and the little golden arrow indicates the day of the month, next to which can be found Sunday Letter, feast days, syllables of the "Cisiojanus", a mnemonic device of 12 verses to help remembering the main feast days in each month. The emblem of Old Town, three golden towers on a red shield, is in the centre of the dial and around it there are smaller circles with 12 signs of the zodiac and bigger circles with depictions of months.

At the end of the 18th century or at the beginning of the 19th century, the clock was completed with the addition of twelve apostles. The original statues were destroyed in a fire in May 1945 and were later replaced.

There are four polychrome moving statues on the sides of the astrological clock. The represent, from left to right, Vanity, Avarice, Death and a Turk. There are two more pairs of statues on the sides of the calendar dial: a philosopher and St Michael the Archangel on the left and an astronomer and chronicler on the right. The 19th century gilded statue of a rooster is the newest of the statues of the clock.

sents the Tropic of Cancer, the gold circle around the globe is the Tropic of Capricorn and the one between them represents the Equator. The gilded sun carried along by the hour hand over the Equator, displays the height of the sun above the horizon in any given moment and on the ring of the zodiac signs it indicates the sun's current constellation. The light blue part of the dial represents day, the ochre part represents dawn on the left and dusk on the right, with black part at the bottom represents night. The circle with zodiac signs divided into four seasons is moving over the dial. The small asterisk on its periphery indicates astronomical time. Its periphery is divided into 72 parts, each corresponding to 5 days, and by the position of the gilded sun one can calculate

▲ *A view of some Old Town Square houses from the tower of the Old Town Hall*

continued from page 77

The tension in Prague grew into street riots and Hus left to find refuge in the south Bohemian Kozi Hradek Castle. He was burned at the stake for heresy in Constance in 1415. The citizens of Prague demanded communion under both kinds and after some chaos and negotiations, King Wenceslas IV permitted the communion in three churches in 1419. The radical preacher Jan Zelivsky, based in the Church of Our Lady of the Snows, became the leader of the followers of Jan Hus, so-called the Hussites. After the outbreak of the revolution and the First Prague Defenestration taking place in the New Town Hall, radical Hussites stormed through Lesser Town, attacked Prague Castle and temporary captured Vysehrad. Despite the heterogeneity of the different Hussite factions, when Prague was in danger from Emperor Sigismund's army, the conservative faction of Old Town united with the more radical of New Town and the Taborit Hussites to defend the city of Prague while it was under attack by the army of Emperor Sigismund. In 1420, Sigismund's crusaders were defeated by the Hussites led by Jan Zizka in the battle of Vitkov Hill and the battle of Vysehrad. Soon, however, ideological and social differences appeared in the Hussite movement. Following internal splits the movement was defeated. The Noblemen's Union, formed by the Catholic and Hussite nobility, in agreement with the officeholders of Old Town, occupied Old Town, Lesser Town and New

Town in 1434. They defeated the last Hussite field troops were in the Battle of Lipany. Thus, at the end of this period, Old Town had a stronger political and economic position than other Bohemian towns. In 1458, George of Podebrady was elected King in the Old Town Hall. Afterwards, a Late Gothic reconstruction of the town hall followed. The west pediment of the Church of Our Lady before Tyn on Old Town Square was completed and its north tower was finished in 1465. After the death of King George of Podebrady, his successor Vladislav II Jagiello founded the Powder Tower near the King's Court in 1479. The tower was built on Royal Road leading from the King's Court to the Castle. King Vladislav II left the King's Court and moved to Prague Castle after some riots in 1485. And once he gained the Hungarian Crown he moved to Hungary (1490).

In 1490, the astronomical clock was repaired by master Hanus. Prague became the leader of the royal towns which were initially against the king and later, paradoxically, protecting the king's power against the nobility. In 1511, the south tower of the Church of Our Lady before Tyn was finished. The significant position of Prague was clearly evident from the inscription above windows of the town hall – PRAGA CAPUT REGNI (Prague, the capital of the Kingdom). It was placed there during the Renaissance reconstruction of Old Town Hall after the end of many years of conflicts between towns and nobility (1520–1528). Prague was temporary united under the leadership of Old Town. In 1539, the Prague Mint was founded in Old Town. However, the resistance of the Old Town,

The House at the Minute at Old Town Square ▲

the New Town and other royal towns against Emperor Ferdinand I and their subsequent surrender, resulted in the loss of numerous privileges and the autonomy of the towns was limited by royal magistrates.

In the 16th century, the imperial court of Rudolf II moved to Prague increasing the prosperity of Old Town. German Lutherans founded the Church of Our Saviour (1611–1614). In 1620, the Church of St Simon and Jude of the Czech Brethren was completed.

Prague lost its privileged political position after the defenestration of the emperor's representatives at the Castle, the defeat of the Czech Estates in the Battle of White Mountain and the Renewed Land Ordinance (1627).

After the Battle of White Mountain, the rebels were persecuted, their properties were confiscated and many were forced to emigrate. The management of Charles University was handed over to the Jesuits. In Old Town Square by the town hall, 27 anti-Hussite leaders were publicly executed after being tortured. Their heads were displayed on the Old Town Bridge Tower for ten years.

In the 17th century, the left bank of Prague was repeatedly occupied and pillaged by foreign troops. However, at the end of the Thirty Years' War (1648) the citizens of Old Town managed to fend off the Swedish, who had reached the Old Town Bridge Tower.

After the Battle of the White Mountain, the members of the town council were exclusively Catholics, thus, the Catholic faith became the only one allowed. In the upcoming Baroque period, the building development was financed mainly by the Church and the nobility. Gothic churches and monasteries in Old Town were renovated in Baroque style. The Dominicans built a monastery by the St Giles (Jilji) Church (1625), the Servites founded a monastery by the Church of St Michal (1627), and the Jesuits built the St Clement's College, the Clementinum (1653–1723) and a boarding school for young noblemen, the Konvikt. The Knights of the Cross with the Red Star built a convent and the Church of St Francis (1661–1688) next to the Charles Bridge. The Carmelite Monastery was built next to St Gall's (Havel) Church (1671) and the Paulians built a in 1684.

▲ *The monument of Jan Hus*

From right to left, the Tyn Church, the House at the Stone Bell and the Goltz-Kinsky Palace at Old Town Square ▲

(33)

▲ *The saxophone player Vladimir Pinta*

The Gothic Church of St Castullus (Haštal) was renovated in Baroque style (1689–1695). In 1715, the Jesuits completed St Clement's Church in the Clementinum and in the following years also the library, the Mirrors Chapel (1724), the Astronomical Tower and the east wing of Jesuit dormitory. The Church of St Nicholas was built on Old Town Square (1717–1730) and the Church of St Bartholomew at the Konvikt (1726–1731). The Baroque decoration of the Gothic St James Church of Friars Minors was completed (1736–1739). Baroque palaces such as the Clam – Gallas Palace (1713–1719) and townhouses were built. Charles Bridge was also decorated in Baroque style.

In 1760, the moat separating Old Town and New Town was removed and a new promenade from the Horse Market to the Powder Tower was created (later called "Ve starych alejich" i.e. In the old allyes). In the 2nd half of the 18th century, beautiful Rococo palaces were erected in Old Town, e.g. the Goltz – Kinsky Palace (1755–1765) e.g. Old Town Square and the Pachta Palace (1770).

The Empress Maria Theresa's reforms, the centralization of political power and the germanization on Czech territory created a better environment for establishment of new scientific and cultural institutions. The first newspapers were issued. The Jesuit Order was abolished by the Pope (1773) and the Clementinum library became accessible to the public. The first public reading room where one could also borrow books, was opened (1781) at the House At the White Unicorn on Old Town Square. The first book print-

ing facility was established in Old Town in 1797 and was later moved to St Agnes Convent. The Classicist Nostic Theatre (today Estates Theatre), where the world premiere of Mozart's Don Giovanni took place in 1787, was built in 1781–1783.

The reforms were continued by Emperor Joseph II by the abolition of serfdom (1781) and the Decree on the merger of four historical towns of Prague (1784), causing the arrival of new residents in the industrial suburbs of Prague. The Old Town Hall became Prague City Council. On the periphery of Old Town, the moat from the Horse Market to the west was being removed. A new boulevard called "V novych alejich" i.e. In the Old Alleys was created and shortly became a new main street and fashionable promenade. was created. In 1839, the construction of the Chain

▲ *The interior of St Nicholas Church*

St Nicholas Church in Old Town Square ▲

▲ *The Tyn Courtyard or Ungelt, the Church of St James the Greater in the background*

The interior of St James Church ▲

Bridge began. Old Town, which had been suffering from floods since the Middle Ages, was to be protected by raising the height of the riverbanks (1841–1845). On the new, higher riverbank, next to the Chain Bridge, the Lazansky Palace was built (1861–1863). It later became famous as the Café Slavia and as the residence of the composer Bedrich Smetana.

In the 2nd half of the 19th century, a new road lined with new buildings emerged at the place of former Old Town moat. Trams pulled by horses began to run on this street in 1875. The Historicist styles on this street were represented, by the Neo-Gothic Powder Tower (1875–1886) on one end of the road, and by the Neo-Renaissance National Theatre Czech Savings Bank (1863–1896), now the Academy of Science, on the other

▲ *St James, facade detail*

end of the road. Many older buildings standing on the place of the town walls, were demolished or renovated. The new Old Town Market (1893–1897) was built near the Horse Market in the place of four demolished houses. New apartment buildings were constructed in Old Town. Nonetheless, the historical centre was still partly industrial. Mills, a print shop, a brewery, a distillery and other workshops were still operating. The constructions on the new, higher riverbank continued towards the bend of Vltava River, where the Neo--Renaissance gallery and music hall called Rudolfinum was built (1876–1886). Rudolfinum had many uses over the years: temporary seat of the Parliament after the Czechoslovak Republic was proclaimed; University of Applied Arts (1885); and present seat of the Czech Philharmonic. A significant change of the core of Old Town was the redevelopment of Josefov (Prague ghetto) and of its surroundings in the late 19th century. About 600 houses were demolished and were replaced by new Art Nouveau apartment buildings in the early 20th century. The high street of this new district, Paris (Parizska) Street, was intended to be on one end of a boulevard, which would have been connected to Wenceslas Square on the other end. However, a new Neo-Gothic wing of the Old Town Hall was built in the way of this 'boulevard-connecting' idea. The elegant Art Nouveau Czech's Bridge was built (1906–1909) and the boulevard was to be continued on the other side of the river. In the middle of Old Town Square the sculptural group of Jan Hus and the Hussites was unveiled (1915). Yet the most important Art Nou-

St Agnes Convent ▲

of Philosophy and the Faculty of Law, the SIA building (Association of Engineers and Architects, later SOF building – World Trade Union Federation, now the Hotel President) and St Francis Hospital (1925–1927) were built between 1928 and 1929. The Cubist Teachers' Cooperative Apartment Houses near the Hotel Intercontinental is definitely worth a look. At the end of World War II, the Neo-Gothic wing of the Old Town Hall was destroyed during the Prague Uprising in May 1945. These parts were damaged: Gothic chapel, astronomical clock and interior of the tower. In the post-war reconstruction, the wing that was burnt down had to be demolished. Only a part of the wall next to the tower was preserved. Since then, various projects aiming to redevelop the empty space have been rejected by the public.

veau building in Prague is the Municipal House (1913) with beautiful Art Nouveau interiors and concert hall. It was erected where the destroyed King's Court used to be. On one side it is connected with the Powder Tower and on the other side it is adjacent to the Art Nouveau Hotel Paris. In their vicinity, on so-called Kings Road linking the Powder Tower and Old Town Square, there is the Cubist-style House at the Black Madonna (1911–1912). Next to the riverbank, the Ministry of Trade and Industry (1932) was built in late Art Nouveau.

In the 1930s new buildings were built in Old Town, such as the New City Hall and the Municipal Library (1926–1930) on Marianske Square. The Faculty

▲ *The House at the Black Madonna, a masterpiece of Czech Cubist architecture*

The Estates Theatre (originally Nostic Theatre and in communist times Tyl Theatre) ▶

PATRIAE ET MUSIS

Les

In contrast, other still vacant or demolished places were redeveloped. At the end of Paris Street, Hotel Intercontinental was built (1968–1974) and in its vicinity the SOF building was renovated in order to house Hotel President. In the post-war period, the Bethlehem Chapel was restored and largely reconstructed (1950–1952) and the building of the Rectorate of Charles University was built anew (1945–1959). In the 1970s, the department store Kotva was built (1970–1975) in the periphery of Old Town near the Art Nouveau.

After the Velvet Revolution (1989), the construction of new buildings in Old Town continued. The Myslbek Gallery was built near the old Fruit Market. The Four Seasons hotel was built on the riverbank. The Stock Exchange Palace was built near the department store Kotva. At the initiative of President Vaclav Havel and the Vision 97 foundation, foundation of Dagmar and Vaclav Havels, the long deconsecrated Church of St Anne, founded by St Wenceslas in 927, was reconstructed. It became an international spiritual centre named "Prague Crossroad".

▲ *The Powder Tower, Celetna Street* *The Municipal House by Republic Square is one of the most famous Art Nouveau buildings in Prague* ▶

▲ *The Mayor's Salon, decorated with murals by A. Mucha*

Jews started arriving in Prague from its very beginning. These originally travelling merchants started settling down in the city from the 10th century. They were mostly Ashkenazi Jews of Central and Eastern Europe. They established settlements in today's Old Town, New Town, Lesser Town and under the Vysehrad Castle. Being savvy marketers, they quickly acquired wealth, which provoked envy and on that account often became victims of pogroms. Moreover, for religious reasons they did not become integrated which later led to exclusion from practising a range of professions. Initially, they were allowed to do professions related to money such as money exchange and money lending.

The first known privileges were granted to Jews by Prince Sobeslav II in the late 12th ccentury and by King Ottokar II in the mid-13th century. Jews had already been living in Old Town and Charles IV allowed them to settle in the newly founded New Town, where a "Jewish Garden" i.e. a cemetery, had already existed. Its remnants were accidentally uncovered in the end of the 20th century during a building development. The privilege of settling in New Town was confirmed by King Wenceslas IV. The status of Jews was at first one of foreigners living in the area with the permission of the king, paying him a tax for it. They were under a par-

The Spanish Synagogue

The interior of the Spanish Synagogue ▲

ticular legal status and were directly subordinate to the king. In disputes between Jews and Christians, matters were resolved by a royal official in the name of the king. In disputes within the ghetto, matters were resolved by a rabbi or Jewish judge. In later periods, the king sometimes granted the privilege of consenting of the settling of Jews to feudal lords outside of Prague, who were also allowed to collect tax for it.

The Jewish settlements in Lesser Town, New Town and under the Vysehrad Castle were parished in the Middle Ages. Jews of Old Town formed a community. The beginning of this community was a settlement around the so-called "Old School". The only reminder of this settlement today is the name of street near the Spanish Synagogue. Another community was also formed in Old

Town around the Old-New Synagogue. However, due to differences in and in social and legal status, Jews were discriminated and gradually became more and more isolated. A ghetto with its own administration was created. Subsequently, Jews had to wear distinctive and discriminatory signs while outside of the ghetto, such as tall hat since the reign of Charles IV and little yellow circle on their clothing since 1551.

Many Jews were murdered in a pogrom in 1389. The philosopher and poet Rabbi Avigdor Kara composed a dirge in memory of the victims which is still being read in the Old-New Synagogue. The rabbi's tombstone (1439) is the oldest in the Old Jewish Cemetery.

In the 15th century, Prague Jews became victims of many pogroms. During the Hussite wars, many were murdered

and the ghetto was pillaged repeatedly even after the Hussite Wars ended and Prague was conquered by George of Podebrady. King Vladislav II Jagiello banned the oppression of Jews in 1499. The Municipal Assembly of the Kingdom of Bohemia endorsed the right of Jews to reside in the kingdom and an annual tax was set for them to pay. The efforts of the Royal Crown to start collecting this tax (so-called royal regal) once again, caused a dispute between King Ferdinand I and the Estates which led to the expulsion of Jews from the kingdom in mid-16th century. After being expelled twice in a short period of time, His Majesty, Maximilian II confirmed in 1567 that Jews could remain in Prague. During the rule of Emperor Rudolf II the ghetto expanded and new houses and synagogues were built. The legend of the Golem was created in these prosperous times of ghetto. Rabbi Jehuda Lev Ben Bezalel had allegedly created the Golem from clay. The Renaissance tomb of Rabbi Lev (Loew) is the best known in the Old Jewish Cemetery.

After the defeat at the Battle of White Mountain, the non-Catholics were persecuted, their assets confiscated and they were forced to emigrate. Jews survived this period by paying various taxes and giving loans to the emperor. A privilege granted to them by King Ferdinand II gave them more freedom and consequent economic growth which caused expansion of the ghetto. The Prague ghetto was almost entirely destroyed by the Black Death in 1680 and

▲ *The statue of Moses in front of the Old-New Synagogue*

fire in 1689, however, was subsequently restored in a relatively short time.

In the 18th century, Prague was repeatedly occupied by foreign armies and Jews were always forced to pay various types of contributions and retributions. During the Prussian siege, the ghetto was threatened even by the citizens of Prague. Jews tried to seek help from the Prussians but they failed and after conquering Prague in 1744, the ghetto was pillaged by the Prussians. Subsequently, Empress Maria Theresa expelled Jews from Prague in 1744 but her intention was not realised. The empress was pressured by the Czech nobility interceding for Jews, since they could not be immediately replaced in the financial sector. The empress permitted Jews to return under several conditions and only after paying a "tolerance tax".

The Enlightenment, the reforms of Emperor Joseph II, the abolition of serfdom, the Patent of Toleration and the merger of the towns of Prague, all meant equal rights for Jews. Jews no longer had to wear a yellow badge and were allowed to practice all professions. The ghetto became an equal part of the city and it was named Josefov. Its walls were demolished and Jews could settle on the outside as well. In 1850 Josefov became a separate district. Gradually, only poorest and Orthodox Jews remained, while the richer left the overcrowded ghetto. Living conditions and the state of buildings gradually worsened, thus, the redevelopment of the entire ghetto and its adjacent areas was agreed on (1893). A new residential area in Art Nouveau style was emerging

The Old-New Synagogue and the High Synagogue ◄

(43)

▲ *The Old Jewish Cemetery*

from the beginning of the 20th century to the beginning of World War I at the place of the demolished ghetto. Its main boulevard was called Paris Street. Out of the original buildings of the ghetto only the most important monuments were preserved, such as the Old-New Synagogue, the only one currently used for religious purposes in the former ghetto, another five synagogues serving as museums, the town hall and the Old Jewish Cemetery.

After the ghetto was demolished some wealthy Jews constructed apartment buildings. Jewish symbols can be found on houses near the Old Jewish Cemetery in streets, such as Siroka and Maiselova. Plans to expand the Old Jewish Cemetery were not materialised and only a Neo-Romanesque ceremonial hall was built. Therefore, a new Jewish cemetery was established outside the city centre. Franz Kafka, who was born in the area of the ghetto and spent almost his entire life in Old Town, is buried in the latter cemetery. During the redevelopment, a new reformed synagogue was built in place of the former "Old School". Its exterior and interior decoration is in Moorish style. The synagogue was named Spanish Synagogue and currently serves as a museum and concert hall.

After the proclamation of the Czechoslovak Republic (1918), the Jewish nationality was recognised and Jews became equal citizens. With the support of the Republic, three congresses of the World Zionist Organization were held in the country.

The period of World War II and the Nazi occupation is a tragic chapter of the 20th century. At the beginning of the war, about 120 000 Jews lived in the territory of today's Republic. In the early moments of the occupation, some managed to legally emigrate in exchange for a high financial investment, others fled illegally later on, but soon after they lost even that option. They were excluded from public life and transported by the Nazis to the empty fortress of Terezin town in the north of Prague, only to be gradually deported to extermination camps. About 80 000 Czechoslovak Jews died during the war. The names of the victims are written on the walls of Pinkas Synagogue in the ghetto and in synagogues in other parts of the country.

The Jewish Museum was founded in 1906 as an effort to preserve monuments from the ghetto. Valuable objects from all over the country, concentrated by the Nazi during the occupation, were preserved as well. In 1994 the museum buildings were returned to Prague Jewish Community and the collections to the Federation of Jewish Communities in the Czech Republic.

The Ceremonial Hall of Prague Burial Society ▲

זה השער לי" צריקים יבאו בך

Carefully planned New Town of Prague was founded by Charles IV on 8 March 1348. Charles IV himself took part in the planning of the town but the plans have unfortunately not been preserved.

Charles IV was crowned King of the Romans in 1346. He became King of Bohemia after the death of his father in the Battle of Crecy, and began to transform Prague into a magnificent city, the capital of his empire. On the next day of his coronation as Czech King, on 3 September 1347, Charles IV laid the foundations stone of the Augustinian Monastery and the Church of Our Lady of the Snows which were only partially completed in 1397 and left unfinished during the Hussite Wars. Its nave is the highest in the historical centre.

Newly established New Town covered an area of about two square kilometres on the periphery of Old Town. Its territory was twice the size of Old Town. In this area outside the Old Town walls, there were already a few settlements, which were later incorporated into the new space within the New Town walls. The intention of Charles IV was not only to create a protective zone for Old Town, but also to unite the two towns. Thus, Prague was to be turned into a city and a centre of trade of Central Europe, due to its strategic location on the

◄ *Jubilee Synagogue*

Wenceslas Square ▲

▲ *The National Museum, the statue of St Wenceslas*

routes between south and north as well as between east and west.

A few days after founding New Town, on 7 April 1348, Charles IV founded a university in Prague, which was the first university in Central Europe. He later initiated the construction of a stone bridge over Vltava River in 1357, which was completed in 1402.

In New Town, main market places and main streets were outlined. All residents of New Town were exempt from taxes for 12 years and were granted the same rights as the citizens of Old Town. In the Charter of Foundation of New Town, Charles IV also specified which crafts would have to relocate from Old Town to New Town in the following year.

The main market squares in New Town were the Horse Market (now Wenceslas Square), the Cattle Market (now Charles Square) and the Hay Market (now Senovazne Square). Wenceslas Square, the centre of Prague today, was constructed perpendicular to the walls of Old Town. The centre of New Town was current Charles Square. In its vicinity, Charles IV founded the most important building of New Town, the Emmaus Benedictine monastery (Na Slovanech),

where Old Church Slavonic was used as liturgical language.

Religious buildings, such as the Romanesque Rotunda of St Longinus and the Church of Apostle Peter, were already standing in the settlements on the grounds of the newly established town. Afterwards, Charles IV gradually founded a number of monasteries and churches, such as the Church of St Stephen, the Church of St Henry and St Kunhuta, the Augustinian Monastery with the Church of the Assumption of Virgin Mary and St Charles the Great, the Benedictine Monastery of St Ambrose, the Church of St Apollinaris and the Church of St Catherine. In December 1367 Charles IV officially unified

The statue of St Wenceslas in Wenceslas Square (Josef Vaclav Myslbek) ▲

Old Town with New Town under a single administration seated in the Old Town Hall. Consequently, he ordered the demolition of the gates and walls separating the two towns and the removal of the moats. The merger of the two towns did not last long. Charles IV annulled the unification ten years later in March 1377 and on that account a large part of the demolition work had not been completed. The New Town Hall on Charles Square was first mentioned in a report from 1377.

▲ *Grand Hotel Evropa at Wenceslas Square*

Lucerna Passage ▲

After the death of Charles IV (1378), during the reign of his son Wenceslas IV, the construction work in New Town still continued but not in the same speed. The Chapel of Corpus Christi, a place of annual exhibitions of the Crown Jewels and relics of saints, was built in the middle of Charles Square. Wenceslas IV briefly resided in New Town, but he soon returned to King's Court in Old Town.

Wenceslas IV was unable to handle the increasing social and religious problems intensified by the arrival of sellers of papal indulgences in 1412 and by the burning of Jan Hus. After Jan Hus was burnt at the stake for heresy in Constance in 1415, Wenceslas IV started indecisive maneuvering between supporting the Catholics and giving concessions to the Hussites, in terms of permitting the practice of Holy Communion under both kinds in three churches. Moreover, the king's brother, Sigismund, started threatening with military action against the Hussites.

In early July 1419, Wenceslas IV appointed Catholic residents to the positions of New Town councillors. On 30 July 1419 a crowd of radicalized Hussites occupied the New Town Hall and defenestrated the Catholic town councillors. The Hussites elected their own new town councillors and Wenceslas IV, shortly before his death, was forced to legalise the election. Soon after this First Defenestration of Prague, the Hussites took over Old Town and the revolution started

Franciscan Garden, the Church of Our Lady of the Snows ▲

▲ *The National Theatre*

to spread. Thus, the construction of buildings in Gothic style in New Town was abruptly terminated by the Hussite Wars. The settlement between the Hussites and the Catholics was announced in the New Town Chapel of Corpus Christi in 1437, after the defeat of the Hussites. In 1455–1456 the tower of New Town Hall was built.

Several attempts to unify Old Town and New Town under a single administration followed, but they were always subsequently separated. Due to the complicated situation in the country, construction work could not continue in the same manner as during the reign of Charles IV.

Almost a century after the end of the Hussite Wars, their adverse outcome was still affecting Prague. The city was recovering slowly. The population decreased (by about 25 000) and commerce was stagnating. The nobility consolidated its position of power over the rebellious towns. In 1500, Prague lost a number of previously acquired privileges. Subsequently, Old Town and New Town were defeated in a rebellion against the king. In the mid-16th century, the citizens of Prague also lost their privileges, the city lost its

▲ *A triga on the roof of the National Theatre*

The theatre curtain by V. Hynais ▲

▲ *The Lesser Town water tower*

autonomy and the royal officials of Ferdinand I took control.

In 1583 Emperor Rudolf II moved with his Court from Vienna to Prague. The economic boom and the influx of foreigners manifested mainly in the vicinity of the Castle. However, even in Old Town rich burghers started reconstructing their houses in Renaissance style. Renaissance affected New Town only marginally.

After the Thirty Years' War, The Baroque style in New Town was represented especially by buildings of the Church. New palaces of aristocrats started emerging by the Old Town walls. In 1636, near the Powder Tower, the Capuchin monks started building the Church of St Joseph. In the same year, Spanish Benedictines from Montserrat, locally called "black Spaniards" due to the colour of their clothe, arrived in the Emmaus Monastery. They renovated it in Baroque style and added spires to the church. At the Cattle Market (Charles Square), the Jesuits constructed a college and the Church of St Ignatius (1658–1670). In 1670, the Baroque statue of St Wenceslas was placed in the middle of the Horse Market (Wenceslas Square). Near the newly founded Ursuline Convent (1674–1678) the Church of St Ursula was

Slovansky Island (Žofín) ▲

The Manes building ▶

▲ *The Dancing Building*

constructed (1699–1704). The remarkable Michna Summer Palace (1717–1720) is one of the most remarkable Baroque buildings in New Town. In the 18th century, several churches were built in New Town, such as the Church of Virgin Mary (1724–1727) in the Elizabethan Monastery, the Church of St Charles Borromeo (1730–1736) and the Church of St John of Nepomuk on the Rock (1730–1739). Although new Baroque fortifications (1653–1730) were erected around the whole Prague, they did not prevent the French or the Prussians from heavily damaging the city in the mid-18th century. In 1773 the Jesuit Order was abolished and public life remarkably changed due to a series of numerous reforms that occurred during the reign of Maria Theresa. Her son, Emperor Joseph II, united the four towns of Prague into a single city by his Decree on 12 February 1784.

Attempts to establish factories, especially textile ones, began in the first half of the 18th century. However, the Industrial Revolution reached Prague only during the 1930s. New industrial suburbs were created and engineering started emerging. New Town was changing rapidly. Prague was growing and New Town became the actual centre of the city. Classical residential and educational buildings were erected in New Town. The very first train arrived in the centre of Prague from Vienna in 1830s. However, despite the growing industry Prague remained a provincial town of the Austrian Monarchy.

In the second half of the 19th century, the city walls were demolished. In place of the demolished walls separating Old Town from New Town, a beautiful boulevard new railway was created. In architecture, Classicism was blending with upcoming Neo-Renaissance. The Neo-Renaissance building of the National Museum was built at the upper end of the Horse Market (Wenceslas Square) and the Neo-Renaissance New German Theatre (now Prague State Opera) was build close to the latter. Other important buildings in New Town, such as the National Theatre, were also built in Neo-Renaissance style. For the construction of the National Theatre (1868–1881) a nationwide collection was organised, indicating the growing Czech national consciousness. Nearing the completion, the Theatre was damaged in a fire but it was soon restored and opened in 1893.

At the turn of the 20th century, a whole range of beautiful Art Nouveau buildings emerged in New Town, such as

▲ *The statue of Jan Evangelista Purkyne*

The New Town Hall ▲

the buildings of Topic Publishing House (1906–1907) and the Prague Insurance Company (1906–1907 near the National Theatre, apartment buildings and the Hlahol Association building (1903) near the river, the Municipal House at the site of the former King's Court (1905–1912) and Hotel Central (1899–1900), Hotel U arcivévody Štěpána (later Šroubek Hotel, now Grand Hotel Evropa) (1905) and Garni Hotel (now Hotel Meran) (1903), the Peterka House (1899), Adam Pharmacy (1912) and Koruna Palace (1911–1912) at Wenceslas Square, the Novak House (1902–1903) in Vod-

▲ *The Church of St Ignatius*

Karlov, the Church of Virgin Mary and St Charles the Great ▶

▲ *Emmaus Monastery*

ickova Street and others. The main railway station was also renovated in Art Nouveau style (1901–1909). The Jubilee Synagogue (1905–1906) was built in Moorish style, a unique style for this time, close to the Gothic Church of St Henry. In 1912, at the top of Wenceslas Square a new equestrian statue of St Wenceslas accompanied by four patron saints was placed. In the early 20th century, new styles appeared in art and architecture. Under Vysehrad Castle, in the area known as Podskali, the first Cubist houses were built. Cubism was popular in Prague until the 1930s.

After World War II, the Czechoslovak Republic was proclaimed in the Municipal House and Prague became its capital city. In 1920 Greater Prague was created by a law prescribing the incorporation of neighbouring towns and villages.

During the interwar period, Constructivism and Functionalism were becoming popular in architecture. The so-called Rondo-Cubism of the post war buildings, such as the Czechoslovak Legions Bank (also Legiobanka, today Archa Palace) (1921–1923) and Adria Palace (1923–1924) can be considered Czech Art Deco.

At the end of World War II, some buildings were bombed in New Town. In the vacant places, buildings of different styles and quality started emerging. The Emmaus Monastery was severely damaged by the bombing but was subsequently reconstructed and modern spires were added on top of the church. At Wenceslas Square, Hotel Jalta (1955–1957) and the House of Foodstuffs were built in Socialist Realism style. In the following years, on Narodni Trida Avenue, the controversial department store Prior 02 (later Máj and today My) (1972–1975) was built as well as the New Stage of the National Theatre (1977–1983) on the centennial anniversary of the opening of the National Theatre. In the 1970s and 1980s, three metro lines were constructed passing under the city centre. During the construction of the so-called North-South Highway North-South highway on the periphery of New Town separating the National Museum from Wenceslas Square the Neo-Renaissance station of Tesnov near the river had to be demolished.

After the Velvet Revolution (1989) some buildings in New Town were renovated and others were built anew. The most famous are the Dancing Building (1994–1996) on the riverbank and the Palladium Shopping Centre built in place of old barracks and opened in late 2007.

The Emmaus Monastery of the Benedictines with the Church of Virgin Mary and the Slav Patrons, called Na Slovanech or Emauzy ▲

I we put aside the prehistoric settlement of this rocky promontory overlooking Vltava River, its history begins in the early 10th century. Several pottery findings and the foundations of a Romanesque church by the later Basilica of St Lawrence have been preserved from the 10th century. Under the rule of Prince Boleslav II, Vysehrad was already a fortress with religious and secular buildings and even a mint. In 1070, Prince Vratislav II moved from Prague Castle to the castle of Vysehrad. He was later crowned as the first Czech King. He founded the Romanesque Basilica of Sts Peter and Paul and next to it a Chapter directly subordinate to the Pope. Being independent from Prague Bishopric, the Vysehrad Chapter kept its important position for a long time. During the reign of Prince Vratislav II, Vysehrad was not only a political but also a cultural centre. In addition to the princely palace, there were other buildings and churches at Vysehrad, such as Church of St Clement, Rotunda of St John the Evangelist, the St Lawrence Basilica whose foundations have been preserved to this day, and the Rotunda of St Martin. The Latin Coronation Gospel, later called Codex of Vysehrad, was

▲ *Vysehrad – a fortress on a rocky cliff on the right bank of Vltava River*

created on the occasion of the coronation of Prince Vratislaus II as King of Bohemia in 1085. Prince Vratislav II was crowned as King Vratislav I but the title was not hereditary. Descendants of Vratislav I resided in Vysehrad until 1140.

During the reign of Prince Sobeslav (1129), the Basilica of Sts Peter and Paul was enlarged and a mausoleum was established in its crypt where King Vratislav I, his wife Svatava and some members of the ruling Premyslid fam-ily were buried. In the late 12th century, the monarchs permanently moved back to Prague Castle. In 1249 the Roman-esque Basilica of Sts Peter and Paul was damaged by fire and the subsequent repairs were carried out in Early Gothic style. In the early 14th century Elizabeth of Bohemia had the basilica enlarged and renovated. The mid-14th century, icon of Madonna of Vysehrad was trans-ferred from the nearby Church of Our Lady of Humility back to Vysehrad.

Under the rule of Charles IV, Vysehrad became a fortified citadel with a Royal Pal-ace and other religious and secular stone buildings. Its fortifications were connected to those of New Town and they had two important gates. There was Sipka Gate, facing the south and leading out of the city, now preserved in fragments. And there was Prague Gate (also called Jerusalem Gate), through which the coronation parades were supposed to pass on the eve of the coronation, on orders of Charles IV.

The interior of the Church of Sts Peter and Paul ▲

▲ *The Vysehrad Cemetery, Slavin*

At the beginning of the Hussite Wars, the Hussites felt threatened by the Vysehrad fortress and so they besieged it and its starving Guard was forced to surrender (1420). Emperor Sigismund rushed to their he arrived too late. The Hussites defeated the Emperor at the gates of Vysehrad. The Hussites, who still felt threatened by it, tore down the walls facing the city, and destroyed and looted the Gothic buildings within. In the subsequent years, Vysehrad was left abandoned for some time. After the Hussite Wars, poor artisans began to settle in the Gothic ruins of Vysehrad since the mid-15th century. Subsequently, the settlement acquired a special privileged position as the Town of Mount Vysehrad. In the early 17th century, the residents of Vysehrad were evicted followed by its renovation as a Baroque fortress which began in 1653 and finished in 1727. Paradoxically, although it never served to protect the city, it was used a hundred years later by occupying forces

Vysehrad park, the sculpture of Ctirad and Sarka by J. V. Myslbek in the foreground ▶

▲ *St Martin's Rotunda is the oldest of its kind in Prague*

(the French 1741–1742 and the Prussians 1744). The casemates of this brick Baroque fortress serve an exhibition area and the largest room called Gorlice is used for exhibiting, original Baroque statues moved here from Charles Bridge. It was being improved as a military fort until the 19th century. It was declared obsolete in 1866, after the Austro-Hungarians lost the war with Prussia. In 1883 Vysehrad became a city district. A short tunnel was constructed in 1903 for the needs of traffic along Vltava River. Vysehrad remained under military administration until 1911.

The 19th century was a period of Romanticism and national revival. Medieval legends of Vysehrad were revived. According to one legend, Vysehrad was founded by Prince Krok. His daughter Princess Libuse foresaw Prague's glory at Vysehrad. Since the male population did not like having a woman as their ruler, she sent out her messengers to bring her a husband. They returned with Premysl, whom they found plowing a field. Premysl became a prince, he was named Premysl Orac (ploughman) and ruled with Libuse from Vysehrad. Another legend tells of Horymir, who had been condemned to death and his last wish was to ride his horse Semik. During the ride Semik jumped over the walls into the river and swam to the other side, thus, saving his master.

We can encounter these and other romantic legends during a walk at Vysehrad. The ruins of what probably used to be a watchtower are now called Libuse's Bath. There are statues of Libuse and Premysl Orac and sculptures from the 1880s and 1890s depicting other legends, all located in the park next to the remains of the Romanesque palace. These statues were taken from Palacky Bridge after World War II.

The Chapter Church of Sts Peter and Paul was renovated in Neo-Gothic style (1885–1893) and in 2003 it was elevated by Pope John Paul II to Basilica Minor in 2003. Its interior includes interesting Art Nouveau frescoes depicting legends and we can see the mid-14th century Gothic painting of Vysehrad Madonna depicting Our Lady of Rain in one of the side altars.

There had been a cemetery next to the basilica since the 13th century and it has been used as a cemetery for people of importance since 1890. Arcades were built on the periphery of the cemetery (1902) ending with Slavin, a joint tomb of eminent personages (1889 1903). The tomb of composer Bedrich Smetana (1824–1884), who dedicated one part of his cycle of symphonic poems called "My Country" to Vysehrad and Libuse, is next to Slavin.

Outside the graveyard, behind Slavin we encounter large mysterious stones, perhaps menhirs. The most famous form a trio called Devil's Column. The Baroque equestrian statue of St Wenceslas from 1678, which originally stood in the middle of today's Wenceslas Square, is in the park near the Neo-Gothic Provostry.

A walk over the Baroque bastions provides us with a beautiful view of the city. One can view the southern suburbs, Prague Castle, New Town and the valley over which Nusle Bridge was built (1973). A motorway runs over the bridge and the first metro line (1974) runs through it.

The Church of Sts Peter and Paul at Vysehrad ▲

The many historical monuments that are located not only in the original four historical towns unified in the 18th century, but especially in the surrounding areas outside of the city in the past and later becoming part of Prague, are neglected by the tourists but also by the government. Unable to list all, we, will mention some of them.

We will start our tour west of Prague Castle and Castle District and will continue clockwise around the historic core. On an elevated plateau known as the White Mountain, a battle took place in 1620, in which the Czech Protestant forces were defeated by the Catholic imperial troops of the Habsburgs. The battle took place near the park Hvezda ie. "Star" and its Renaissance Hvezda Summer Palace (1555–1557). This interesting building in the shape of a six--pointed star was designed by Ferdinand the Tyrolean. From the battlefield towards the Castle District, we encounter the oldest Benedictine Monastery in Bohemia, the Brevnov Monastery, founded by Prince Boleslav II and St Adalbert in 993. Its Baroque Basilica of St Margaret was built in the early 18th century. After winning the Battle

of White Mountain, the Catholics built a pilgrimage site in this area called Chapel of Virgin Mary.

In the north lie the Orechovka district with villas from the early 20th century and Dejvice district with a number of buildings in the style of Socialist Realism constructed in the 1950s. The most significant of these buildings is the Crowne Plaza Hotel (former Druzba then Čedok, Hotel International and Holiday Inn) (1952–1954). Behind Stromovka, the former Royal Park, the Château Troja (1679–1685) was built in the style of Roman villas.

On the way from north to east we encounter Romanesque churches built in settlements that were once located outside the city, such as St Wenceslas Basilica at Prosek completed in 970 and reconstructed in late 12th century and the Church of St Bartholomew in from the mid-13th century.

If we move closer to the centre, we encounter the Negrelli Viaduct, a railway bridge over Vltava River from mid-19th century. Near the bridge, on the left bank lies the building complex of Prague Market (originally the municipal slaughterhouse in 1893–1895), while on the right bank by New Town, lies the district

▲ *Detail from a Troja Palace staircase*

The Troja Palace ▲

of Karlin with its Neo-Romanesque Arcidiaconical Church of Sts Cyril and Methodius (1854–1863). Behind the church rises the Vitkov Hill, where the Hussites had defeated the Crusaders in 1420. The National Memorial was constructed in the 1930s and are located together with the equestrian statue of Hussite leader Jan Zizka of Trocnov on the top of the Vitkov Hill.

In the east of the centre, behind the National Museum located at the upper end of Wenceslas Square, there is the district of Vinohrady which was developed at the turn of the 20th century. The last World War II battles of Prague took place in front of the Radio Palace, only few steps behind the National Museum, during the Prague Uprising in May 1945. The Czechs fought against the Warsaw Pact forces in August 1968 also at the same place. In the middle of the main square of Vinohrady we encounter the Arcidiaconical Neo-Gothic Church of St Ludmila (1888–1893) and close to it the Art Nouveau building of Vinohrady Theatre

▲ *Brevnov Monastery, the Church of St Margaret*
◀ *Hvezda Summer Palace*

The Church of St Bartholomew in Kyje ▲

(1905–1907). A bit further to the east we can see the unusual Church of the Most Sacred Heart of Our Lord (1928–1932) in George of Podebrady Square.

Towards the south, the Constructivist Church of St Wenceslas in Vrsovice (1929–1930) is worth mentioning. The southern outskirts of Prague are known for its Pruhonice Palace that was, reconstructed in Neo-Renaissance style in 1889–1894, and with its park founded in 1895 and with now protected by UNESCO. On the left bank of the river, we encounter the Zbraslav Palace, originally a Cistercian monastery founded in 1292 and the first burial place of the Premyslids.

Towards the centre, in Smichov district, we encounter the late 17th century Baroque Villa Bertramka, where W. A. Mozart used to reside, and the Neo-Romanesque Church of St Wenceslas (1881–1885). Returning to Prague Castle, we can see the late Classicist Kinsky Summer Palace (1827–1831) at the foot of Petrin Hill.

▲ *The statue of Jan Zizka of Trocnov on Vitkov Hill*
The Church of the Most Sacred Heart of Our Lord by Slovenian architect Josip Plecnik in George of Podebrady Square ▶

Prague World War II, expanded mostly in the peripheral areas while the four historical cities remained unaffected. After the Socialist Realism brick buildings, housing estates made of concrete blocks started appearing on the periphery of the city in the 1960s. At the end of the 1960s replacing the previous Socialist-Realism-brick-building style. and in the 1970s, the centre of the city started being penetrated by buildings made of poured concrete. Their effect on the city's architecture was brutal and so this new style was named Brutalism. This style is represented in Old Town by Hotel Intercontinental and Kotva department store. While Castle District, Lesser Town and Old Town were spared of new construction work (except constructions related to the subway), several new structures of New Town, such as the Maj department store, New Scene of the National Theatre and North-South highway, were raising a controversy among the professional and public circles. The construction of the TV Tower began but it was completed in 1991 after the regime had changed. After the Velvet Revolution a construction boom followed. New hotels, office and administrative buildings, shopping centres, apartment buildings

▲ *Kavci Hory Residence*

▲ *Detail from the decoration of Zizkov Tower by David Cerny*

The Zizkov TV Tower ▲

▲ *Main Point*

and new roads were constructed. Peripheries of Prague started to overflow with new housing estates and suburban towns were being filled up with new family houses.

New Town, out of the four historical towns of Prague, was the one most affected by the new building development. However, not all them reach the quality of the Dancing Building by architects Frank O. Gehry and Vlado Milunic, completed in 1996. New buildings were built also on the periphery of Old Town but they rarely crossed its border (e.g. Myslbek Arcade, Stock Exchange Palace). In Old Town, close to Charles Bridge, the new building of the Four Seasons Hotel was built. External changes on the left bank, in Lesser Town are significantly smaller. Mere modifications of existing structures took place (Sova's Mills, Liechtenstein Palace, Herget Brickyard, Kampa Park), while Castle District remained intact.

People interested in modern architecture can find a greater concentration of these structures in three areas outside the historical centre. One is on the left bank of Vltava River in Prague 5 near Lesser Town, where a building complex was erected in place of a demolished factory Vagonka Tatra Smichov, called Golden Angel by French architect Jean Nouvel.

The second area is of the centre, close to Vysehrad, in Prague 4 Pankrac, there was an attempt to develop high-rise buildings all over the area. This would completely destroy the beautiful panorama of the city visible from Prague Castle. After this plan was rejected, several "moderate" buildings were constructed instead. Modern office buildings were built along the North-South highway leading to the motorway towards Brno. The third area is located in the east of the city centre on the right bank of Vltava River, in Prague 8. The O2 Arena, a multi-purpose hall for sports and cultural events, was constructed in place of the demolished engineering factories of CKD. The newest buildings in Prague 8 were constructed closer to New Town. A building near the Hilton Hotel Atrium called Main Point (designed by DaM and finished in 2011), was named the best office building in the world by the prestigious MIPIM Awards. There are other interesting modern buildings nearby, such as Danube House (by New York studio KPF), Amazon Court, Keystone (completed in 2012), Diamond River, River Gardens, Rohan Business Centre and a few blocks away the remodelled factory complex called Korzo Karlin.

Twenty years after the Velvet Revolution, architects began attempting the constructions of new, attractive and unconventional buildings in the city's historical centre. The failure of such projects appears to have been caused by the disagreement of public and professional circles. Thus, long-discussed projects, such as the construction of a new building for the National Library in Letna locally known as "Octopus" and the construction of the Novomlynska Brana building in New Town, have not been materialised.

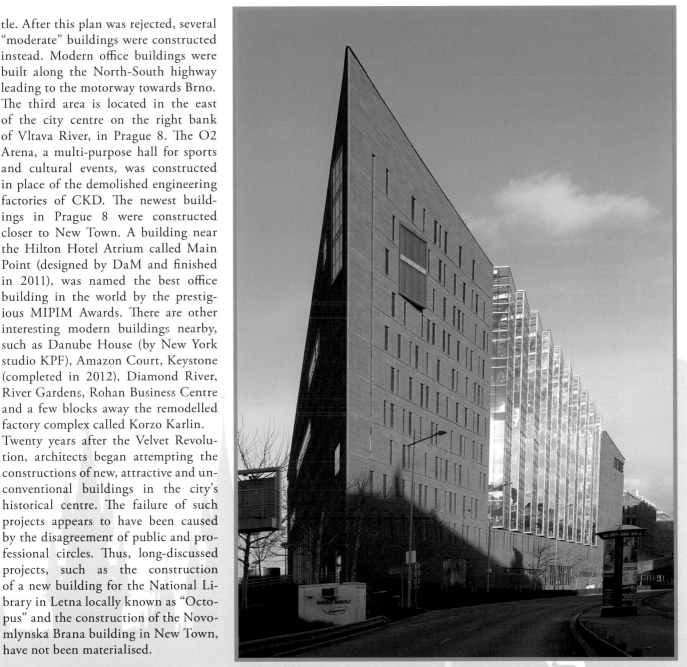

Danube House ▲

PRAGUE

jewel in the heart of Europe

publisher: Daniel Pinta
photography: Daniel Pinta
texts: Ivan Henn
graphic design: Martin Lacina
translation: Bubulina Spanosova, Nela Hakr
illustration: Alois Křesala
print: Tiskárna KALIBA
contact: danielpinta30@gmail.com
contact: Daniel Pinta 00420 777 829 953, 00420 775 979 614, Gabriel Pinta 00420 605 816 362

ISBN 978-80-7528-011-4